DISCARD CLOSE TO THE LAND

REFLECTIONS ON RE-CONNECTING

JIM BYFORD

OUTDOOR TENNESSEE SERIES
JIM CASADA, SERIES EDITOR

THE UNIVERSITY OF TENNESSEE
PRESS / KNOXVILLE 37996-0325

The Outdoor Tennessee Series covers a wide range of topics of interest to the general reader, including titles on the flora and fauna, the varied recreational activities, and the rich history of outdoor Tennessee. With a keen appreciation of the importance of protecting our state's natural resources and beauty, the University of Tennessee Press intends the series to emphasize environmental awareness and conservation.

Copyright © 1999 by The University of Tennessee Press / Knoxville.
All Rights Reserved. Manufactured in the United States of America.
First Edition.

The paper in this book meets the minimum requirements of the American National Standard for Permanence of Paper for Printed Library Materials.

∞ The binding materials have been chosen for strength and durability.

All of the photographs were taken by the author.

Printed on recycled paper.

Library of Congress Cataloging-in-Publication Data

Byford, Jim, 1943–
Close to the land : reflections on re-connecting / Jim Byford. — 1st ed.
p. cm. — (Outdoor Tennessee series)
ISBN 1-57233-029-5 (pbk.: alk. paper)
1. Nature. 2. Human ecology. 3. Natural history. I. Title. II. Series.
QH81 .B9985 1999
508—dc21
98-25371

To Mom, Dad, Uncle Robert, Mr. Walter Hunt, Daryl, and Brad and Julie

Contents

Editor's Foreword	IX
Jim Casada, Series Editor	
Preface	XIII
Acknowledgments	XV

Part I. Re-Connecting

Slowing Down	3
Bounty from the Land	9
Spending Time Outdoors	30

Part II. Seasons

Spring	45
Summer	53
Fall	65
Winter	76

Part III. Animals Make the Land Interesting

Patterns among Animals	85
Tales about Mammals	93
Tales about Birds	102

Part IV. Understanding the Land

Through the Eyes of Children	123
How the Land Works	131

Part V. Taking Care of the Land

Stewardship	147
Final Thoughts	169

Editor's Foreword

When I first read the manuscript of *Close to the Land,* the words immediately reminded me of two writers, both with Tennessee connections, whose work I have long admired. One was a sporting scribe from the glory days of outdoor writing two generations ago who has subsequently become almost a cult figure, Nash Buckingham. After taking an undergraduate degree from the institution which is publishing the present work, "Mr. Buck" (as he came to be known to his wide circle of friends and admirers) spent most of the remainder of his long life in Memphis.

In many senses Buckingham's years were filled with unending wonder, because he devoted his life to bird hunting and waterfowling, field trials and dog training. The experiences, in turn, provided him with the raw material from which he crafted the enduring tales found in books such as *The Shootinest Gent'man, Mark Right!* and *Hallowed Years.* Nonetheless, his was not the life of privileged leisure many suppose. In his later years especially, the specter of poverty haunted Buckingham and his beloved wife, and he always regretted the financial circumstances that made him a virtual prisoner of the home he and his wife had in the heart of Memphis.

As he once confided to his dear friend John Bailey, "daylight and darkness come differently in the country." Buckingham was a man who cherished the land and its creatures in a fashion few urban dwellers can, and one feels a deep sense of sadness in the realization that a man to whom the good earth meant so much enjoyed far too few sunrises and sunsets in solitude, as opposed to observing them amidst the unseemly hustle and bustle of the city.

Mr. Buck was an individual who would have been a companion to Jim Byford's heart, and the same certainly would have been true of the second writer Byford's volume brings to my mind. The late Harry Middleton's book *The Earth Is Enough* conveys in its title and even more in its contents sentiments strikingly similar to those found here. That work, destined in time to become a minor classic, has its setting in the Ozarks, but Tennessee figures prominently in Middleton's second book, *On the Spine of Time.* Again, this time using his affection for angling in the Smokies as a medium through which to praise the virtues of communion with the wild world, Middleton reminds us that nothing is more satisfying and soothing to the soul than hours spent in direct contact with nature.

At the outset in *Close to the Land*, Jim Byford echoes the same strong, meaningful message that provided both Buckingham and Middleton ongoing inspiration. "I can honestly say," Byford writes, that "I've never met a piece of land I didn't like." To him, modern lifestyles are dangerous, far more hectic and fast-paced than the relaxed, predictable rhythms of the natural world. Byford is a staunch advocate of the importance of moving in concert with those rhythms, savoring and sensing each season in turn through the simple process he describes as "re-connecting."

In the pages that follow you will find a powerful, sometimes poignant, and ultimately persuasive plea to reestablish closer ties with the earth. Byford urges us to maintain close touch with nature, pausing and pondering the endless myriad of wonders which await the watchful eye and receptive heart.

In essence, this work comprises a series of impressionistic vignettes. They are organized in a sensible scheme, one redolent of the sort of practicality which has always characterized those who live close to and wrest their living directly from the earth. After opening with strong advocacy of reconnecting with the land and suggesting how this can be accomplished, Byford turns to the ebb and flow of the seasons. Too often those of us who live in this part of the world fail to appreciate the fact that we are privileged to enjoy four distinct, evenly spaced seasons, each with its special charms. Byford captures the essence of what makes each season singular, and he does so in a fashion reminiscent of the writings of the great Canadian natural historian and fellow lover of the land, Roderick Haig-Brown. Haig-Brown chose the medium of fishing to do this, in his quartet of books entitled *Fisherman's Spring, Fisherman's Summer, Fisherman's Fall,* and *Fisherman's Winter*. Byford casts his net wider, but the end result is just as pleasing.

The work next turns to creatures, great and small, and some of their entrancing and distinctive habits. You soon realize that the material you are reading comes from long, quiet hours spent in observation and contemplation, and to join the author as he walks along wildlife paths is to tread trails of wonder. Fittingly, the concluding sections of the book gently guide us toward a fuller, richer understanding of the land. We come to recognize that as knowledge grows so will devotion to the sacred duties of protection and preservation Byford calls stewardship.

While this work certainly conveys an overriding theme, with love of the land being the sparkling thread running through its entire fabric, it also belongs to the genre sometimes described simply as "bedtime companions." These are books which offer a bit of soothing mental sustenance that calms the troubled mind and eases the tired body into sleep. To do so, a book has to be both pleasant and meaningful. Books by Nash Buckingham, mentioned above, fall into this category, as do those by other southern sporting scribes such as Robert Ruark, Havilah Babcock, and two earlier contributors to the Outdoor Tennessee Series, Gary Cook *(Oakseeds: Stories from the Land)* and Sam Venable *(From Ridgetops to Riverbottoms)*.

Byford tells us, and rightly so, that this is a collection that permits readers, should they be so inclined, to sample the book "in short stints" and with "frequent naps." After all, these offerings are the product of a lifetime of observation and a strong, ever-strengthening love affair with the land. They represent two decades of literary craftsmanship (portions of the work previously appeared in the *Southeast Farm Press*) and, more than that, a heartfelt outpouring from a passionate lover of nature and all its wonders. They deserve to be read at a relaxed pace in keeping with the pulse of the land that forms their subject.

When Jim Byford says "come with me and share my soul," it is an invitation no one who shares even some small portion of his feelings should ignore. He reminds us, in a simple, satisfying fashion, that we are "critters" too, and that, like all life, our very survival as a species depends on respect—indeed, reverence—for the waters which form earth's life blood, the air that partners these waters, and, as Byford implies everywhere, on loving the land.

Byford's book, in its thrust and tenor, might well have been a lengthy statement of purpose for the Outdoor Tennessee Series of which it now becomes a part. It extols the virtues upon which the series is predicated, and anyone who truly loves the land, whether in Tennessee or elsewhere, will find reaffirmation of that love here. They will do so through the delights of armchair adventure as they join a staunch son of the Tennessee soil in a moving tribute to the land which holds his heart in thrall.

Jim Casada
Series Editor
Rock Hill, South Carolina

Preface

Whatever we do, we do for some reason. Often, it's money; sometimes it's fame or glory. When I was young, I often did things to please my parents. My incentive for writing this book is quite different. For one thing I have always wanted to write a book, just for the adventure of it. But more than that, I want to share, with anyone who will listen, my appreciation of the land. I want you to witness, even if it's secondhand, some of the thrills and adventures I've had in the outdoors. If you enjoy reading the trailing of my humble pen—if you can enjoy some of my adventure—if I can make you feel some of the fondness I have for this glorious land of ours, then my labor will have been worthwhile.

This book is written differently than most. Instead of flowing in continuous thought, it is rather a collection of essays and short stories—some of which are new, but many of which I have written over the last twenty years. Many were originally published in the *Southeast Farm Press* between 1984 and 1998. You can read in short stints and take naps often, if you like, without losing your way.

I can honestly say I've never met a piece of land I didn't like. Compared with some folks, my travels have been limited—but then again, I've seen quite a lot of territory. And from ocean to desert, from prairie to rainforest, from river bottom to the high mountain volcanic ash, I have appreciated it all.

I often hear people describe a piece of land as barren, as desolate, and even as a wasteland or biological desert—but I've never known such a place. I have never seen land devoid of life, even if I had to scratch around in the soil a little to find it. Wherever God is present there is life, and where there is life, His ecological tapestry is there for the trained eye to see. And I've never seen a place without it—I hope I never will.

So come with me and share my soul. I hope you enjoy reading as much as I've enjoyed writing!

Acknowledgments

I am thankful for the blessings in my life and for who I am. I'm thankful for my happiness and for my continual quest for adventure. I'm thankful for my family and my sense of order and stability. I'm thankful I know the land and for my relationship with it. I'm thankful, and I owe much to many.

In appreciation, I thank these people, to whom this book is dedicated:

Mom, the first love I ever knew, for giving me birth and understanding me, for helping me see the good in life, and for helping give me perspective.

Dad, my hunting and fishing buddy, for introducing me to the outdoors, for taking me there even when he didn't have time, for teaching me right from wrong, and for sharing with me his common sense.

Uncle Robert, the best business teacher I ever had, for showing me the wisdom of taking care of the land.

Mr. Walter Hunt, my vocational agriculture teacher, for helping me discover who I am and showing me the path to reaching my potential.

Daryl, my wife and partner, for showing me the value of family and giving me one to love, for the fortitude and determination of holding our marriage together through the tough times, for patience as I grew up, and for overlooking my excesses.

Brad and Julie, my son and daughter, for being great kids and forgiving me for not always being there for them, even when I gave others more time than them, and for loving me in spite of my tunnel vision.

My special close friends, with whom I've shared my love of the land and many campfires.

And, finally, I thank God for holding my hand when I was weak and for showing me the path to a full life.

Re-Connecting

Slowing Down

Like all species, we are products of cell union and division—created with a genetic likeness to our parents. Our very existence and continued survival depend on the land and its resources. Unlike most species, we have created an artificial habitat into which our resources are now piped in from distant places. It's easy to forget the land, from which our sustenance comes, especially when our needs are met so plentifully and efficiently. Instead of foraging, as did our ancestors, we busy ourselves making our surroundings even more artificial. The more conveniences we have, the more we believe we can accomplish. We continue to cram more activity into our lives, to the point that we find ourselves going at breakneck speeds. Such is the fodder of stress, ulcers, and heart attacks. Meanwhile, the natural world deliberately eases along at a steady, relaxed pace—much the same as our ancestors experienced it. It pays to visit the natural part of our world often, so we can re-connect; that is, to be reminded of how we're probably "supposed" to live.

Take Time to Smell the Roses

Mac Davis had a hit song several years ago called "Stop and Smell the Roses." We could learn a lot from that song—"Did you ever take a walk through the forest, stop and spend some time beneath the trees? You can look up through the leaves right straight to heaven, and you can almost hear the voice of God in each and every breeze."

A number of my friends have had heart attacks in the last few years. Some have died, and some survived their second or third attack. Many of them are in their forties—younger than I am. I'm well aware it could happen to me, too. When it comes to life and death, there are no guarantees when and where they will happen.

We're learning more about heart problems every day. We know they usually result from a combination of genetics, eating improperly, lack of exercise, and abuse of certain drugs, including tobacco and alcohol. We also know that stress is a major factor. Now, none of these factors alone will cause a heart attack. It usually takes a combination of excesses. Obviously, we can't do much about our genetic background, but we can control the other factors.

In many ways, stress is harder to control than the other factors. Stress is not all bad, though. Some stress improves job performance and keeps us on our toes. It's when we have too much stress that it becomes deadly. A lot has been written on ways to minimize stress, but I'll leave a discussion of that topic to the experts. What I want to talk about is the value of taking the time to stop and smell the roses.

When was the last time you stopped for one minute—sixty seconds—during the waking day and allowed your mind to drift or to focus on your natural surroundings? When was the last time you tuned out the TV and tuned in to the natural world? Stop right now and try it. Put down the book, go outside, close your eyes for one minute, and listen to the natural sounds. Now, open your eyes and focus on anything natural—up close. Great, isn't it?

Have you ever counted the number of minutes in a day? I'll save you the time. There are 1,440, and everybody has the same amount. You can use yours however you wish. Most people who have stress rush to cram as much activity into that 1,440 minutes as they can. Most people who have heart attacks from stress feel that if they're not active every waking minute, they're wasting their time. I wish to differ. Taking time to relax improves performance. People who relax not only have a better chance of preventing a heart attack, but they can be more productive in less time.

You know, we spend a lot of time and money on teaching our kids. But in some cases it would be better if we let them teach us a thing or two. Youngsters who don't constantly have a TV in their face will find interesting things to do. If they're outside, in the natural world, they're watching a spider build a web, an ant colony gather food, or a bird build a nest and feed its young. Children take the time to stop and smell the honeysuckle and passion flowers. We rob them of their time. How many times have you told your kids, "Come on, we're going to be late. Hurry up, you'll miss the bus. Get away from that pile of dirt; you'll get your clothes dirty." We rush them away from what they are learning in their natural world, so we can teach them to become as stressed as we are.

There are some adults who spend all their time smelling roses. Then there are those of us who never stop building and navigating a social structure. There's no question we need structure, for without it, society would be in chaos. On the other hand, our world can be too highly structured, and we're proving that every day as more people die of stress.

It's interesting that the people who wake up as adults and realize that stopping to smell the roses *is* productive time are usually the ones who have been warned by a heart attack. Before the attack, they felt their job couldn't go on without their constant diligence. They rushed faster to get farther behind, and then were made aware of their mortality through a heart attack. Maybe youngsters have something to teach us after all. Maybe there's some merit to Mac Davis's song.

CROWDING CAUSES STRESS

It's always good to come back home, no matter where you've been. But when I've been to a large city, coming back to my rural West Tennessee home has special meaning. A few years ago, I was in Washington, D.C., for four days. Not that Washington is worse than any other big city—it's not. In fact, in many ways it's better than most. The Metro subway system is very efficient and inexpensive, once you figure out how it works. The beltways are nice, too, as well as the feeling of pride that sends a tingle up your spine as you visit the many historic sites.

But like all cities Washington has the familiar symptoms of overcrowding—symptoms of stress. As my wife, Daryl, and I were leaving the airport for our hotel, the shuttle driver, a young woman, got that glazed look in her eye—the same look as a gladiator going into battle. With clenched jaw, she took the offensive, cutting off other drivers, honking to warn some, and yelling to tell others to get out of the way. When she changed lanes to turn, she dared others to ram the van as she nosed, dived, lurched, and sped in and out of traffic. I watched her more than I watched the traffic. The only time she lost that glazed, cool, determined look, she actually laughed out loud at a couple of drivers in front of us who were shouting and gesturing obscenities at each other. I could tell they were enraged, even though I can't understand Spanish.

Mostly, people I encountered in Washington were cool and distant, if not rude. Occasionally one would smile at my southern accent. My wife has a way of getting on the friendly side of folks, though. When she took the time to talk with them awhile, they would gradually lower their guard, smile, and talk a little.

Washington shows the same symptoms of crowding as do other large cities I've visited—north, south, east, and west—all over the United States. Chicago, Atlanta, New York, and San Francisco all have one common problem—too many people living too close together cause stress to people who live there. They're stressed from the minute they wake until their head hits the pillow. Some continue to worry all night and don't sleep well. The drone of traffic, the flashing neon lights, the frustration of stepping in a neighbor's pet deposit, and the insane pace of rush hour start the morning on shaky ground. The cursing from a boss for being five minutes late, when it wasn't your fault that the dumb traffic was snarled. The grunts and sneers of hungry customers who are in a hurry because they're late for work. The shortage of help who don't care whether they work or not. On and on and on ... but there are few friendly voices and faces, no space, no quiet, no natural sights and sounds, no time to relax—all things we in rural, small-town America take for granted.

Anyone who's spent time in both kinds of places can relate to what I'm saying—it's very obvious. Don't get me wrong. There are stressed people in small-town America and calm ones in large cities, but the general patterns are clear. Several studies have actually documented these stress-inducing phenomena. The classic study was done many years ago. A scientist set out to monitor stress behavior in a rat colony subjected to increasing levels of crowding. The study was designed to measure only one stress factor—lack of space. A pair of rats were placed in a container with plenty of space, food, and water. They were calm and seemed content. As the pair reproduced and the colony grew, food and water were increased to accommodate the additional animals, but space was not. As the colony grew, the animals became more and more stressed and were less tolerant of one another. The stronger, younger rats chased the older, weaker ones away from the plentiful food and water. They "badgered" the disadvantaged, the pregnant and suckling mothers and the baby rats. Behavior of the young rats was described as being similar to juvenile delinquency in teen-aged people. Mothers stole nesting materials from each other—and in general there was chaos in the colony. When the researcher doubled the space, stress was noticeably reduced and order was soon restored. As the colony continued to grow (food and cover were still abundant, but space was not), the old pattern of stress symptoms began to reappear, and, indeed, history repeated itself. Studies of people in crowded conditions have shown similar results.

City residents are aware of these problems, of course, and many city leaders are trying to correct them. Parks, beltways, suburban homes, and public transportation are a few of the things being tried. But reducing stress in such situations is hard to do. One thing is for sure: you can never make a large city as unstressful to live in as a small rural community. It's sure good to be home.

On Natural Time

Up until a few years ago, I had never lived close to an area where I could hunt deer. When I was a graduate student in Alabama, I lived in deer country, but never had a good place to hunt close by—whenever and however I liked. When I did hunt, it was as an invited guest, usually on a dog hunt, and then only occasionally. When I moved to Georgia, I had to drive 60 miles to hunt, and when I lived in Knoxville, I had to drive 240 miles to get to good deer country.

Out of necessity, I evolved into a deer hunter/camper. I mostly camped out of a pickup truck in the woods. When I went deer hunting, I planned to stay at least three or four days, sometimes longer. I always dreamed of living in a place where I could hunt near the house, a place where I could hunt for a few hours in the morning, go into work, and then maybe hunt a few hours before dark. Now I live in such a place. I have several good hunting spots close to home—places with just as many deer as my former distant spots. And I take advantage of them, just as I always dreamed I would.

But it's not the same. Something's missing, and it took me about four years to figure out what it was. What's missing is the opportunity to slow down to "natural time." You see, there's natural time and human time. With natural time, there's no rushing here and there—no meetings to make nor classes to teach. The natural world just drifts along at a steady, reasonable pace. Some critters get up at dawn and go to bed at dusk. Some move intermittently all twenty-four hours, but get plenty of short rest breaks in between. Squirrels scurry around when they're hungry, but after they eat their fill, they stretch out on a limb and nap in the sun. Deer stop every hour or so, lie down, and chew their cud.

But in human time we're always rushing around during the day and half the night. FAX machines, cars, computers, microwaves, and telephones all save us time, but time for what? Time for more meetings, more work, and more commitments. Even when we play, we rush to fill those precious hours. Sometimes, in fact, we're more tired after playing than after working.

When I travel several miles away from home or the office to hunt, I generally hunt for three or four days at a time. I take enough time to slow down to natural time. It usually takes me at least a day of hunting to gradually slow down. Instead of ignoring the little details and distractions of human time (such as traffic, billboards, and incessant noise), I begin to notice small things.

I catch little flickers of movement and tune in to subtle sounds and smells, just like other predators. It's only then that I become an efficient hunter.

A three-and-a-half-day bow hunt a few years ago stands out in my mind. It wasn't very far from home, but far enough that it wasn't practical to drive home each day. And what a wonderful hunt it was! I slept out under the stars and made sawmill coffee from spring water. I swapped tales around a campfire with my good friend Mike, with whom I've hunted for many years. We listened to great horned owls, barred owls, and screech owls, which were interrupted occasionally by howling coyotes. I went to sleep to the soothing murmur of a nearby stream and awoke to a bright moon in a star-studded sky—bright enough to transform tiny droplets of dew to a million jewels strewn across the meadow. There were no telephones, TV's, or radios to litter my mind with news of the human world's worries. There were no worries in this natural world I found myself in—at least none that seemed important at the time. No, everything was all right. Life began to take on a new perspective, and priorities seemed to fall in line. It seemed more natural to relax and soak in the grandeur, to reflect on how people are supposed to fit into the scheme of things—not alone in the human world, apart and often at odds with the natural world, but as other organisms living in harmony with the natural world, with their own special niche to fill.

After having achieved my objectives of securing a little venison for the freezer and re-creating my mind and body (and also after running out of time), I grudgingly packed up and headed home. But in the corner of my mind, the campfire still flickers and the stars still shine. That memory will have to do for now, until I can head back to the woods and slow down—to "natural time."

BOUNTY FROM THE LAND

Anthropologists tell us that humans have roamed the earth for a million years, and for 990,000 years they all gathered the food. The strongest hunted wild game, and the rest gathered wild fruits, nuts, leaves, roots, and succulent plants. A short 10,000 years ago, humans discovered agriculture—the art of planting and cultivating crops and raising animals in captivity. They stopped roaming and began settlements, and thus civilization was born. Since not everyone needed to hunt and harvest, the ones who didn't made technical advances and taught them to others. As farmers became more and more efficient, the rest of society gradually lost the vital connection with the land that hunting and harvesting had provided—the source of their sustenance. Today in the United States, only 1.6 percent of us farm, and most of the other 98.4 percent are at least two generations removed from the land.

The longer we're away, the less we remember. We're no less dependent on the land today than we ever were, but America's agriculture is so effective that our awareness of that dependence is dulled. We have become a complacent people, often rebuking the efforts of those who manage the land—the farmers, the loggers, and others who feed, clothe, and shelter us.

Primitive humans were aware—their daily existence depended on it. They watched the weather not because rain would foil their picnics, or because snow would inconvenience their travel, but because their very lives were at stake. They were keenly alert as seasons changed—had they not been, they may not have survived until the next season. In the United States, Native American cultures were perhaps the last to live more or less in harmony with the land; European settlers brought a civilization that didn't.

Native Americans of yesteryear weren't always conservationists in our modern-day sense. According to historical accounts, they were sometimes wasteful, but as a rule they respected the land and its resources. If they hadn't, they wouldn't have survived. For example, hunters in many Native American cultures held a quiet ritual after harvesting a wild animal from the land. Kneeling beside a fallen deer was followed by a silent prayer of thanks to the spirit-that-moved-through-all-things, or a ceremony that resulted in thanking the animal for giving its life so the hunter and his family could survive the coming winter. Nearly every part of the animal was used: antlers for knife handles; tendons for bowstrings and for tying stones to wooden sticks for arrows, spears, and axes; skin for clothes, quivers, and tepees; bones for awls and toys; brains for tanning hides; and fat for food and grease to reduce friction. They ate all the meat, some fresh and the rest cured in the sun and stored for later use. They ate most of the internal organs, but used

In our sophisticated world, human knowledge is abundant and profound, but most adult humans are as ignorant of their connections to the land as a fetus is completely unaware of the umbilical cord through which its sustenance comes. These two squirrels taken with a .22 rifle will make a nice meal for this predator and his wife.

some for other things—bladders, for example, were often used as canteens. Blood and the rest of the organs were used as fertilizer for what little corn and other crops they planted. Some parts, such as hooves, bones, and pieces of antler, were used for good-luck necklaces and other trinkets, so the spirit of the animal's swiftness and wariness would always be with them. In short, they recognized the worth of the animal and appreciated its life. When they decided to take a life, they made sure it was not wasted.

Primitive cultures were connected to the land that provided their sustenance, and they understood the connections. We're just as dependent on the land today, but most modern humans don't understand the connections. In our sophisticated world, human knowledge is abundant and profound, but most adult humans are as ignorant of their connections to the land as a fetus, dependent on its mother, is completely unaware of the umbilical cord through which its sustenance comes.

Today, hunting is not necessary for human survival in most cultures. Yet the instinct to carry out the ancient predator–prey ritual is still alive in the modern sport hunter. Some hunters don't fully understand why they hunt. Others of us have thought it through, and choose to keep alive and even cultivate the predator–prey instinct. That instinct becomes weaker in a society that, generation by generation, moves further from its connections to the land. Although most hunters don't know it, the desire for a "trophy" set of antlers probably is a throwback to the days when our ancestors proudly displayed bear claws and other parts of strong, wise, or older animals to prove to their village that they had the stamina, cunning, or swiftness to take that animal. Unfortunately, hunting competition and commercialization have clouded the real reason most of us hunt—to stay connected to the land.

As we move into the twenty-first century, competition and commercialization of hunting are not the real concern. The real concern is ignorance in our modern society of how dependent it is on the land and its resources. With that ignorance comes the risk of society placing less and less importance on wise use and management of those resources. Things upon which we place little value tend to get shoved aside. Our greatest hope is to create an awareness among our children of their connection to the land—adults are too hard to teach.

To Hunt—Or Not?

A few years ago, I had the opportunity to talk to a group of young people—and their adult leaders—about the philosophy of hunting. It's an interesting topic. I'm an avid hunter and have been all my life. But when I speak to young people, I have a deep sense of responsibility to be as honest as I can, because they can be easily swayed. When I'm totally honest with them—and myself—I have to admit there are some things about my sport that turn me off, not about the true sport itself, but some attitudes among some of my fellow hunters.

You know, when I grew up, things seemed a lot simpler. When we needed meat for the table, mom would go out into the yard, catch a chicken, wring its neck, and we'd have chicken for supper. We'd kill hogs in the winter and put the meat up in the smokehouse. Nothing seemed wrong about it—not then, not now. Since most of our young people only see meat in the store, and never see the animal it came from, it takes some effort to make them understand. Many grow up without ever understanding hunting, and from this group of young adults springs a growing number of anti-hunting and animal-rights activists. On the other side are the hunter activists. And there's a rather large group in the middle—those who aren't yet sure. This is the group that will ultimately decide the fate of sport hunting. Let's look at some of the arguments the anti-hunters are using.

Slob hunting. If hunting is truly a sport, what about those hunters who have no respect for landowners' property? Abuse on the land by four-wheel-drive vehicles, three- and four-wheelers, snowmobiles, and the like is rampant. Deep ruts in farm roads and fields, which kill vegetative cover and cause extensive erosion, have no place in any "sport." Riding down fences, leaving gaps down and gates open, littering, and shooting at signs are as much acts of vandalism as writing on rest room walls. Not all hunters do this you say? Only a few? Maybe so, but why is it that posted "No Trespassing" signs are spreading like measles across the countryside?

Macho hunters. If hunting is such a great sport, why is it that grizzly guys with blood-stained hands, boots, and pants will sometimes think nothing of sitting down in a restaurant beside a family with kids who don't understand? Have you seen the mud-spattered pickup on stilts with a deer draped across the tailgate—meat spoiling in the sun? Have you heard hunters bragging about "sticking one" or "knocking that sucker down with a running 200-yard shot—took about 5 shots, but I got 'im?"

Materialism, gadgetry. Hunters talk about sport. What's the sport in running a bear with dogs and converging on him with three pickups equipped with two-way radios, scoped rifles, and a cooler full of beer? How many hunters could kill a deer if the only equipment they had included a hunting knife and longbow? What is the future of any "sport" where gadgets replace knowledge and skill?

Trophy hunting. Maybe hunting was justified when all the meat was eaten, hides were used for clothing, and antlers for handles, buttons, and farming tools. But when the only objects hunters seek are antlers to brag about, something's wrong.

If you're a hunter, you may be getting pretty mad about now. Before you fly completely off the handle, think. Sure, there are some things anti-hunters don't understand. But isn't it true that all these activities and attitudes do occur within our sport? It's certainly true that not all of us behave this way, but some of us do. Some of us don't seem to have much regard for the taking of an animal's life. And I don't know about you, but that bothers me.

Early in my deer hunting career, I once saw a deer in the throes of death. Due to the circumstances, I couldn't dispatch it quickly, and the experience of watching it suffer left a sadness etched in my memory I can't forget. I vowed after that to hone my skills so my future killing shots were quick and humane.

Why do you hunt? If you don't know, or if it's for the wrong reason, I suggest you ponder a bit. I know exactly why I do. The reason is long and complicated, but, simply put, I am a predator. All of us are born with a predator instinct. Some ignore it and it eventually goes away—just the same as the innocence of our childhood. But some of us cultivate that instinct. I don't apologize for that, any more than I apologize for cultivating the instinct for survival. But like the Native Americans, I feel a sadness with the passing of my prey. It lasts only a moment, then I feel triumphant that I was once again able to provide meat for my table. Yes, I too like to take big-antlered deer, because they are difficult to harvest and that usually means my skills as a hunter are still honed. But taking a doe or a younger animal means my skills are still intact, too—at least to a degree.

Be patient with those who don't understand. They only love animals, while true hunters both love them and enjoy cultivating the predator instinct. And remember: wildlife belongs to *everyone!* This is one of the brightest aspects of the New World. No longer do the wealthy own wildlife—that's one of the reasons we left Europe. Your hunting license gives you the right to hunt, but wildlife belongs to everyone until you harvest it—then it's yours. Also remember that even though landowners don't own the game, they own the right of access to it. Whether you pay for that access or it's given to you, treat it with respect.

Self-Confidence

I was mesmerized as I watched each raindrop form on the tiny twig in front of my nose, and one by one drop twenty-five feet to a soaked forest floor. With the exception of an hour-long lunch break, I'd been sitting in the treestand all day. It was about forty-five minutes before dark and I hadn't seen a deer. Matter of fact, I hadn't seen much of anything except rain. It seemed for the moment that everything alive was under a shelter, except me. I had thought more than once about dedicating the day to ducks and retreating to more civilized quarters. But deep down I had this feeling.... Suddenly, a sixth sense told me to look up. And there he was—a beautiful ten-pointer!

The confidence that caused me to stay put until the last possible moment has helped me put a lot of meat on the table and build a storehouse of memories. That confidence didn't come overnight, though. When I first started deer hunting in the early sixties, there was no one around to teach me. My dad had taught me how to hunt squirrels, but there were no deer around in those days. The skills I'd honed from squirrel hunting were priceless, but they alone weren't enough to bag a deer. I hunted deer for three years—hard—before I killed one. Before I harvested that first deer, I constantly had doubts; I simply couldn't visualize it happening. After the first one, though, I had no problem. Once I started expecting to kill a deer every time I went out, I began taking at least one deer every year.

My dad is an excellent squirrel hunter, with an eye for movement in the woods as keen as a Cooper's hawk. But he hunted deer for over twenty-five years before taking his first. The problem? He didn't have enough confidence to hunt long enough, be still enough, or look hard enough. Over those twenty-five years, he began to believe that deer were super smart and super wild. He quit deer hunting a couple of times—even sold his gear—but I'd pester him until he'd start back again. And then one day it happened.

My dad is an excellent squirrel hunter, with an eye for movement in the woods as keen as a Cooper's hawk. But he hunted deer for over 25 years before taking his first. Loyd G. Byford with his first deer, in the early 1980s.

After sitting for an hour watching a hillside, he got up and started moving around. He glanced back at the hillside, and there, in broad open daylight, as big as life, stood a legal deer. Later, he relayed that while he was dragging that deer back to camp, another legal deer stepped out, and had his tag not been filled, he could easily have bagged it as well. Well, Dad went on to kill five deer in as many years. They no longer seem super smart to him—in fact, now he's amazed at some of the "dumb" things he's seen them do. The only difference is that Dad now has confidence. One important thing to keep in mind is that you can't see deer if they're not there: in the early years when Dad and I first started deer hunting, there weren't many deer around. It hasn't been until the last couple of decades that deer-restoration programs have caused deer to flourish.

I know lots of other folks who went through several lean years until they gained confidence in their abilities. That's not just true about deer hunting either. Bass fishing, trout fishing, fly fishing for bluegills, elk hunting, and duck hunting all require a great deal of learning and confidence building. Probably the king of confidence shakers is the eastern wild turkey. To bag a wild turkey, you have to do everything right. You have to understand the bird, its habitat, and possess basic hunting skills. On top of that, you need to have confidence that you can kill one—and *on top of that*, a little luck sure is helpful!

As with everything else that's worth doing, overconfidence can be as bad as lack of confidence. Let me give you an example. Early one fall, after I had taken two deer with a bow, each with a single arrow, I was getting pretty sure of myself. Not only did I expect to take a deer every time I went to the woods, but I had also pretty well patterned the deer. I "knew" what time a certain buck would come by, which direction he would come from, and the angle and distance of the shot I would take. You see, I had already seen him three times and moved my treestand to the right spot. Sure enough, at 10:30 A.M. this beautiful fall morning, he appeared just the way he was supposed to. He spent the right amount of time feeding under the big oak with the crooked limb, then moseyed over toward the other big oak at the head of the hollow. He would pass within fifteen yards of my tree; I would let him pass 'til I got the quartering away shot I wanted, and then it would be over. I was so busy deciding how I would process him (let's see, my wife needs this one mostly ground, but he's young enough to have good tender steaks . . .), it never occurred to me that he was passing at ten yards instead of fifteen. You can guess the rest—one more lesson in humility. Oh well, that's what makes hunting the sport it is.

In recent years, I haven't measured the success of the hunt by pounds of meat I've put in the freezer. Far from it. But I have to say that knowing I have a *good chance of taking game* contributes to my enjoyment of hunting, and keeps the sport exciting. And that knowledge comes from confidence—pure and simple!

Cooking Wild Game—Keep It Simple

"There is no vertebrate in North America that is not edible, except some box turtles—and these only because they sometimes eat poisonous mushrooms. And, unlike deer and rabbits which also eat them on occasion, box turtles metabolize the toxin more slowly, often accumulating it in their tissues." I remember well this statement from one of my professors many years ago. However, contrary to what many people think, of the approximately seventeen hundred species of birds and mammals in North America, only about one hundred of these are considered game and are hunted for food. For these one hundred species of game, there must be thousands of recipes, many of which are excellent, and many I wouldn't feed to my dog—unless I apologized first.

Preparing game is as simple as preparing any other meat. Many cultures have known this for years—cultures that depend on wild game as their only meat source. My wife taught me that underlying truth many years ago, and it's the one I use to teach folks how to cook wild game. I don't pay much attention to wild game recipes. Each species of wild game is similar to some species of domestic animal. For example, bear meat is most similar to pork, deer to beef, grouse to chicken, etc. Once the similar domestic meat is identified, wild game can be cooked using the *same* recipes and cooking methods used for the domestic meat. It's that simple.

There are a few basic principles that apply. First, we should understand the various groupings of wild game meat. For example, birds that are migratory (for example, doves) have dark breast meat that tends to be tougher, because of the long flights they take, as compared to nonmigratory birds (for example, quail), which don't exercise their breast muscles through flight very often. The meat is dark from the many blood vessels needed to supply oxygen to the heavily exercised muscles. Quail and turkey legs are dark for the same reason. Some mammals, like squirrels, are lean with very little fat, and others, like raccoons, are fatty. Some fish (especially trout), reptiles, and amphibians are meaty, and some are rather bony (like rattlesnake). Cooking methods for birds—especially dark-breasted birds—should be those that maximize moisture, such as slow-pot cooking, pressure cooking, braising, microwaving, etc. Another principle is that all fat on game should be removed, because if there is ever an "off flavor," it will usually come from the animal's fat. Most wild animals with fat during certain times of year generally have it mostly on the outer part of their bodies, just under their skin. This fat can be easily removed by the cooking process. The easiest way to remove fat from game is to bake it in an oven on a drip tray, so the fat can render through the porous tray to the pan at the bottom and later be discarded. Once the fat is rendered out, the meat can be barbecued, put in stews, or used in other ways. Any fat needed in the recipe should be provided from similar domestic meat. I seldom use fat at all.

The "wild taste" people normally associate with game meat is often caused either by fat left on the meat or by the meat being treated improperly. Another principle, then, is that all meat, whether game or domestic, should be cleaned, dried, and cooled right after killing. An "off taste" or "wild taste" is caused by bacteria growing on the meat. Bacteria have to have moisture, warmth, and food to grow, so the carcass should be dried out inside the body cavity (all blood and other surface moisture wiped away), and the meat should be cooled as soon as possible. It's not necessary to hang the meat for several days before butchering, even though hanging will tend to tenderize the meat somewhat. Taste does not seem to be affected, whether or not the meat is hung in a cooler. Often hunters, trying to hang their meat for several days in a barn or garage, will allow it to get too warm during the afternoons, causing slight deterioration, and thus the "wild game" taste.

Wild game meat is not only delicious, it is also higher in some nutrients than domestic meat, and lower in fat as well (3 percent compared with 30 percent, in some cases.) In fact, some weight-loss programs that place restrictions on the amount of beef or pork in the diet place no limit on the amount of game meat eaten.

So, consider wild game the true delicacy it is. It tastes expensive, but costs nothing. (You get to write off the cost of the hunting trip to recreation!) It's nutritious, yet delicious. But throw away your game recipe book and unplug your computer. The secret to fixing wild game is *keep it simple.*

Venison: Lean, Healthy, and Tasty

I remember well the first deer I ever saw. I was 18 years old when I saw two does at Chickasaw State Park. They were truly beautiful animals, with all the grace and agility I'd read about in the frontier books. After I killed my first deer three years later, my family savored every morsel of the meat. After that, I killed deer regularly. My wife used to joke that our son Brad would probably grow deer antlers, he ate so much venison.

Sadly, most folks today take venison for granted, because deer are now so common. Deer relocation efforts and herd management in various states—combined with the uncanny ability of deer to survive and adapt—have brought deer from the brink of extinction to plentiful numbers. In Tennessee alone, we harvest well over one hundred and fifty thousand deer every season—and as the harvest goes up each year, the population continues to grow. Tennessee's harvest every year conservatively nets over nine million pounds of edible venison.

This is good meat. In fact, for the increasing numbers of health-conscious folks, it offers the best low-fat meat. Consider the following comparison of 100 gram portions:

	Calories	Protein (grams)	Fat (grams)
Choice Beef (trimmed)	301	17.4	25.1
Med. Fat Pork (trimmed)	308	15.7	26.7
Venison	126	21.0	4.0

My family loves the taste of venison, and that's about all the red meat we eat. But everywhere I go I hear people say they don't like it. After talking with them awhile, it's easy to see why. They don't treat it like other meat. The keys to preparing good venison are, for the most part, the same as for preparing good beef, pork, etc.: 1) keep it fresh, cool, and clean, 2) don't soak the taste out of it with brine or vinegar, and 3) don't add any special spices or seasonings you don't like just to "hide" any preconceived idea you may have about the taste. In other words, treat it as you would any other good piece of meat—with a couple of possible exceptions: 1) throw away all deer fat; if you want fat, add beef or pork fat, 2) because the meat is mostly lean and has little water, it should be cooked slow and moist with low heat. Use cooking methods such as slow-pot cooking, braising, pressure cooking (save the juices!), roasting-pan cooking, etc.

Back during the days before refrigeration, our forebears either canned or dried their food. This not only allowed them to store it, but also permitted them to carry it with them on long trips in hot weather. Venison jerky was often prepared by the early pioneers to carry while hunting, because it provided a lot of energy and protein in a relatively small package. I have been experimenting with some ways to make venison jerky and have found the following method successful:

Cut lean strips of venison (fresh or thawed) in pieces one-quarter to three-eighths inch thick and about five inches long. Loin, fillet, round, and flank are often used; tender meat gives a better product.

Make a brine of one-half lb. salt to 1 gallon water and store in a granite canner, stone crock, or plastic bucket. Add meat. Weight the meat so the liquid covers the entire surface and allow to stand for twenty-four to thirty-six hours.

Remove the meat and *lightly* rinse with fresh water.

Sprinkle the meat moderately with sugar.

Place it on a broiler tray and sprinkle *lightly* with one part caraway seed, browned in the oven and ground, and two parts curry powder. Broil about ten inches from the coil for about twenty to thirty minutes, turning the meat as needed.

Remove the meat when it is mostly dried, and smoke it in a covered charcoal grill as follows:

Place a small pile of charcoal in one corner of the grill and light.

After soaking hickory chips for thirty minutes, place these chips on the well-burning charcoal, completely covering the pile of charcoal.

Place the jerky strips away from the heat in the far corner of the grill and smoke for two to three hours.

Both top and bottom vents should be about half open.

Let the jerky cool and hang for a few days in the open air (you can hang it from a nail in an open-mesh bag.)

Store in an airtight container. Enjoy!

Caring for Fish from Hook to Pan

After Mom died, we sold the homeplace and helped Dad find a cabin on the Tennessee River. His boat, now on the water in a slip, is ready to go fishing whenever he is. Over the years as I was growing up, I knew Dad loved to fish, but I never knew how much until now. He'd always worked hard and never had a lot of time to fish, but now in retirement, fishing is his life: he goes nearly every day when the weather is suitable. For Dad, taking care of and storing fish is a big deal, because he eats so much of it. Taking care of fish should be a big deal to all of us who love to catch fish and prepare them so they taste good.

Spoilage (even slight spoilage) causes fish to taste strong, or "fishy," and spoilage is caused by bacteria. Fresh fish has no odor—bacterial decomposition causes the strong odor and bad taste. Bacteria need three things to survive: moisture, heat, and food. To minimize bacterial action, we need to remove one or more of the things they need to survive. The bacteria's food in this case is fish, so we need to look at moisture and heat—and heat is the most practical thing to remove. In other words, keep fish cool.

I start by putting fish in an ice-filled cooler, right off the hook, and I keep them on ice until I dress them. Dressing can involve filleting, skinning, or scaling. After washing, they can be frozen, salted, or canned—but if I'm hungry, I cook them right away.

In *The Compleat Angler,* Izaak Walton describes how to dress rough fish so they taste good. Because rough fish have less blood than game fish, and because blood gives any meat its taste, he suggests the following. Scale and wash the fish, then draw the entrails and gently wipe out the cavity. In other words, don't wash after the cavity has been opened, because many of the tiny blood vessels are inside the cavity.

For freezing, many folks put the fish in a container and freeze it in water. I don't like this method, because it softens the flesh—I prefer it firmer. A few years ago, a University of Tennessee study on freezing doves showed that meat tastes better after vacuum-packed freezing. An easy way to do this is to lower a freezer bag three-quarters filled with fish into a five-gallon bucket filled with water (this also works for frog legs, doves, etc.). By lowering the bag completely except for the lip, the water pressure forces all the air out. A good seal then vacuum-packs the meat for freezing.

As mentioned earlier, moisture is one of the things which causes bacterial action. So removing moisture is another way to preserve fish. When I was in Brazil, I noticed the natives drying large fish fillets on top of their houseboats. They sliced the fillets thin so they would dry quickly, before bacteria had a chance to grow in the warm sun.

Salting is another preservation method, partly because salt draws moisture out of the flesh, and partly because most bacteria can't survive in a saline medium. If you want to salt your fish, clean and wash it thoroughly, scraping off scales and slime. One teaspoon of vinegar in a dishpan of water will help remove the slime. Cut the fillet thin as you would to dry it. Scatter a layer of salt over the bottom of a container and place a layer of fish, flesh side up. Keep the layer as even and compact as possible. Completely cover each layer of fish with salt, then place another layer of fish. Repeat until the container is almost full. The last layer should have the skin side up, and finally cover it with salt as well. Put a weight on the fish to make sure it stays under the brine, then cover tightly, leaving it in for ten to fourteen days. You can leave it longer if it's in a cool place. You may wish to repack the fish in a more convenient wooden or plastic container by layering with salt in the same way. Use only one pound of salt for each ten pounds of fish for this repacking. To use, soak overnight in clean water, then cook in a conventional way.

An old man I used to fish with saved all his fish, no matter how small. He would say, "They're as big as butterbeans, and I eat butterbeans." He saved them by canning, and he called the process "making sardines out of them." First, cut the fish into jar-size lengths. Put a teaspoon of salt into each pint-size jar. Fill the jar with fish, packing solidly, and leave one-quarter-inch of space at the top. Exhaust or steam for ten minutes by placing open, filled jars on a rack in a pressure cooker with about two inches of boiling water in it. With a clean cloth, wipe off any grease, sand, or flesh from the jar top so the jar will seal. Set lids in place and tightly screw the jar ring by hand. Put sealed jars on the rack in the cooker with two inches of boiling water. Put the cooker lid on and seal it, with the valve open for five to seven minutes. Close valve (check canner instructions), wait until the needle indicates ten pounds of pressure, then hold that pressure for 110 minutes. After

110 minutes, turn off the fire, but don't open the valve. Let the needle return to zero, then open the valve. Loosen the cover by tilting the back edge of the lid to keep steam away from your face. Remove jars, but don't tighten screw bands. Set them on several thicknesses of cloth—don't set in a draft or on a cold, wet surface. Label them and store them in a cool, dry place, but not where they can freeze.

So there you have it. By taking care of your catch, you can enjoy fish for months. True, it's hard to beat fresh fish, but then again, most of us don't want to fish during the winter. My dad—well, he's the exception.

COOKING FISH

There are lots of ways to prepare fish for the table. Ask any cook and they'll tell you the "best" way. I like fish prepared about any way—except one, a way I tried in Japan. Don't get ahead of me here; I'm not referring to raw. Actually raw fish or sushi is not that bad, because they serve it with a very tangy sauce. Before I went to Japan, I decided beforehand two things: 1) I was going to try every kind of food they served me (I figured I could eat it if they could), and 2) I was going to eat everything with chopsticks, the way they do (actually, they eat soup with a giant spoon and use their hands for some things I might not.) I succeeded on both counts. At one dinner party, though, a man who was introduced as a local politician (he was the only overweight person I met there) took a "special" package out of his coat pocket. He wanted us all to try it. I noticed a guy next to him making a face that in any language says "You've got to be kidding me!" When he opened it up and passed it around, I knew why. It smelled like three-day-old hog manure. About one out of three dinner guests tried it—so did I. It tasted just like it smelled, like I imagine three-day-old hog manure would taste. Turned out, it was fermented fish. Among the many things I learned in Japan, one was that I don't like fermented fish.

When it comes down to it, I prefer my fish cooked, like most everyone else. How folks prefer it cooked seems to depend on where they're from. Down south, most folks prefer fish dipped in milk, rolled in crumbs, flour, cornmeal, or a combination, then deep-fat-fried. The key is to have fat so hot it sizzles the meat when it's dropped in. The pot should be deep enough for the fish to sink below the surface, then float to the top when done. Though any kind of meat or vegetable fat will work, peanut oil is probably the best. Fish can also be fried in a skillet with a small amount of fat—it has to be turned often.

I prefer fish cooked with less fat, and there are several good ways. One simple way is to bake it on a tray in the oven. I prefer it battered as mentioned earlier, and then baked for a crispy, no-fat morsel. Some prefer it baked with butter, salt, and pepper.

Another good way to cook fish is to smoke it on a grill or in a smoker. To make good smoke, soak hickory chips overnight, then put a handful over (but not too close to) the fire. Put the fish over the smoke, but not directly over the heat. On a regular grill, put the fire and chips in one corner and the fish in the opposite corner. You can put the fish directly on the grill surface, or in an aluminum foil tray with butter, salt, and pepper. Some people add vegetables as well. If you don't like the smoked taste, you can simply leave off the hickory chips.

I also like to cook fish over or in a campfire. I've threaded fillets on a stick and cooked them like hot dogs, and I've sealed fish, butter, salt, and pepper in aluminum foil and placed the package directly in the coals. One of my favorite ways is as follows. Take a freshly caught mess of trout ("mess" is southern for about the amount you're craving), clean them in the same stream they came from, salt and pepper them, roll them in flour, and fry them with a little margarine in a small skillet over a campfire built next to the stream. I've paid big money in fancy restaurants to get good food and great atmosphere, but no restaurant has ever come close to this.

People prefer many different kinds of food with fish. Folks in the South seem to like white beans, hush puppies, and fried onion rings with their deep-fat-fried fish. Some like boiled vegetables and rice with baked, grilled, or smoked fish. I discovered one of my favorite scenarios when I was doing deer research in south Alabama. For three months, I lived in a hunting cabin on stilts on a Native American midden mound in the middle of a 250-square-mile swamp. I had to motor four miles by boat from the nearest landing to get to the cabin. I worked with deer at night, then slept in the morning and early afternoon. About two o'clock I'd get up, jump in the boat, and go fly-fishing for bluegills. I'd fry bluegill fillets for supper (that's a southern evening meal) with green beans, black-eyed peas, corn fritters, and hot coffee. Now, friends, that's hard to beat!

CARP TASTES GOOD

You know, I'm amazed at what people think is—and is not—good to eat. Most folks shudder at the thought of eating groundhog or beaver, two species that grow in a clean environment and eat only clean vegetation. Yet, they think nothing of eating livestock, some grown in foul-smelling conditions. Most livestock today eat clean grain and forage, but several years ago, many ate household slop and garbage. It is socially acceptable to eat raw oysters (simply crack the shell and slurp them out), or salted fish eggs (caviar), or drink rotten grape juice (which, after all, is what wine is). But, when we talk about eating crows, snakes, morels, starlings, or other natural delicacies, most folks turn their nose up.

Now, take carp for instance. Most people consider carp a trash fish. In fact, one common recipe for carp that is passed around at cocktail parties is 1) clean the fish, much as you would any other fish, but maybe wash it a few more times, 2) place it on a tray and salt it, 3) put it in the oven at 300 degrees for an hour, 4) take it out, throw the fish away, and eat the tray. Good story, I'll have to admit.

We Americans are reluctant to try things we don't think will taste good. This has come from years of society's conditioning. Carp has a reputation of being oily, tasteless, and grainy, but most people only guess about its taste. We see carp growing in muddy water and deduce that it must not be tasty because of the conditions it lives in. The problem with that belief is that often carp live in crystal-clear lakes, streams, and rivers. And many things we do like to eat grow in worse conditions.

Carp go all the way back to 550 B.C. In the Orient, it's considered one of the very best fishes to eat. In Japan, it has been used in place of money—the larger the fish, the more it's worth. In England, it was a leading game fish, second only to trout. And in many European countries, carp costs more on the menu than steak.

The Asiatic carp was introduced into Europe in the early 1200s. In 1872, 83 fish were shipped to the United States. However, only 5 carp, 6 inches long, lived to arrive. From these 5 fish, the entire U.S. waters were populated. Now, they can be found in just about any freshwater stream, lake, or river in the United States. Carp can grow quite large, up to 55 pounds, but the average is about 8 to 10 pounds.

Carp spawn in the shallow waters of lakes when the water temperature reaches the mid-sixties. They will also begin to move up into the streams when the water warms up a little. In the early spring, they are quite easy to kill with a bow and arrow. Since they are not considered a game fish, any number can be taken—but, if you're going to kill them, be sure to eat them. Living things need not die just for the sake of target practice.

Carp are also one of the fightingest fish we have in southern waters. A large carp can make you think you hooked the Loch Ness Monster. To fish for carp, fish on the bottom and leave the line slightly slack. A number of baits can be used, including earthworms, doughballs (made from rolled-up pieces of hamburger bun), corn, and many other things you might fish for catfish with. If you use corn, you can save money by buying shelled corn and softening it overnight in a little water. The hook easily penetrates the soft midportion of the kernel.

There are many, many carp recipes. Here are just a few suggestions that should work without fail. First, fillet your catch. Marinate the fillets in a mixture of salt, onion, vinegar, and pepper for one hour; then fry to a golden brown. Another way is to dip the fillets in a combination of egg, milk, salt, and flour and then cook them until golden brown in a deep-fat fryer. If you want to bake it, score the fillets with a knife, add strips of bacon, and bake for about 45 minutes at 350 degrees. Baste occasionally with lemon butter. To broil, lay the fillets in a shallow, greased broiler pan, sprinkle with salt and pepper, and spread the tops of the fillets with mayonnaise and lemon juice. Broil in a preheated broiler two inches from the heat for 10 minutes. Some gourmet chefs suggest frying carp after they have been dipped in beer and drained before rolling in flour. Others have steamed carp over a shallow pan of beer under a tight-fitting cover. They suggest steaming for 10 minutes and serving hot in tomato sauce. You may also can, pickle, or smoke carp. One other excellent way to cook it is to grind it, press into patties, and fry it.

The main thing about carp is not to be afraid of it. It's a good-tasting, excellent fish that grows large, is easy to catch, and makes for healthy eating. Oh, and give it a chance, by keeping the fish fresh and not letting it spoil in the sun. No fish tastes good that way. I hope you give it a try this spring.

Tanning Your Hide

No, I'm not talking about what my dad did to me when I misbehaved. I'm talking about the calls I frequently get on home-tanning wild animal hides, especially deer. As hunting season rolls around, you may find yourself asking the same questions.

There are several ways to tan hides. Native Americans used oak bark, ashes, and animal brains. (Squaws chewed the skins to make them soft, but they tell me this is out of fashion now.) Some of the more modern ways involve chemicals that are often hard to find. I'm going to tell you about one method that involves materials you can get at any drug store, supermarket, or building-supply store. The whole process—here goes:

Skinning. Skin the animal in the field—at least while the carcass is still warm. A skin on a cold animal must be cut away, which greatly increases the risk of damage to the hide. For most mammals, a skin can be removed from a warm carcass in a few minutes with practically no knife work needed. Scrape the skin carefully to remove flesh and fat.

Storing. Once the skin is removed from the animal, rub two to three pounds of salt on the flesh side. Be thorough and don't spare salt. If you need to store skins for a while, keep them in a cool place and don't allow them to become wet. Don't put them in plastic bags, and don't pile them on top of one another, unless you add a *generous* layer (about one-eighth to one-quarter inch) of salt on the flesh side of each one. If you stack them on top of one another this way, place them on a wooden pallet so the moisture pulled out by the salt can drain. Without salt, the hides will generate heat and thus cause bacterial action. Once the hair slips (that is, it can be pulled out of the hide easily), the skin is ruined and must be thrown away. (Of course, if the lime/hair-removal step described below is used, the hair will slip, but the skin is not damaged.) Another way to preserve the skin is to freeze it. For freezing, a plastic bag is fine to use, and salt is not necessary.

Hair Removal. If the skin is to be tanned *without* the hair, the next step is to remove hair. A) Soak the skin in a strong milk of lime solution. B) Put six to eight pounds of *unslaked* lime in a wooden bowl or plastic garbage can. C) Add one quart of water *slowly* and stir—*don't let the solution splash on your skin or eyes.* D) After slaking is complete, add two gallons of cold water, mix, submerge the hide, and cover the container. E) Test the hair each day; when it can be rubbed off, the process is complete (about three days for a deer hide). F) Remove the skin and scrape in the direction of the hair with a putty knife or another dull-edged tool. Wash out all traces of lime with fresh water. *Skip steps A through F if you don't wish to remove the hair.* You are now ready to tan the skin.

Tanning. Scrape off any flesh or fat you may have missed. Dissolve two pounds of alum in some hot water. Put five pounds of salt in ten gallons of water, add the alum solution, and mix until it is thoroughly dissolved. Soak the skin in this solution—six to eight days for deer and two to three days for smaller animals. You can't overtan the skin using the alum-salt process, so it is better to leave the hide in too long rather than risk undertanning it. Stir the solution *at least twice a day* to make sure it reaches all parts of the skin. Take the hide out, drain it, and rinse it well in running water. If it tastes salty to the tongue, wash it some more. Hang it hair side out for one to two days in the *shade* over a wooden pole. Turn it and let it hang flesh side out for one to two days until dry. Dampen the skin with a sponge and lukewarm water—don't wet it. Fold it up flesh to flesh, roll it in a piece of burlap, and let it sweat overnight. Work the skin for about twenty minutes—pulling and stretching it in every direction over the edge of a board (flesh side down) to soften it. Apply a mixture of equal parts sulfonated neatsfoot oil and water, warmed and mixed, to the flesh side. Work the skin again over a board until it is soft and dry. Work the skin really well—if it is now oily, remove the excess oil with sawdust, or wash with cold water and detergent. Dry the skin and work it soft again. The tanning process takes time, but these step-by-step directions are easily followed, and you will have a hide you can be proud of.

Common Wild Foods

I've never had to "live off the land," but I believe I could—if the location were fields and forests of the southeastern United States. Most of what I know about the outdoors comes from experience, and most of my experience has been in this part of the world. My formal education has helped me interpret what I've learned the hard way, but as far as knowing what wild foods to eat and how to prepare them, that's come gradually from time afield.

There are many edible wild foods in the southeastern United States, and several complete books have been written on the subject. I'm certainly not an expert in this area, but I know enough to get by, and I've learned what's edible by trying it, if not by making complete meals from it. Here are some of the things I've eaten—most are common enough that you shouldn't need a field guide to help you identify them.

Fish and Game. I've tried about every game and fish species in the Southeast (and a few critters not considered game, such as rattlesnake, bobcat, otter, starling, armadillo, etc.). Some meats taste better than others, but the way meat is prepared has more to do with its taste than the meat itself. Beaver (my wife and I ate twenty-eight one year), muskrat, rattlesnake, crow, and armadillo are especially good, but most folks wouldn't think so. At wild game dinners I've attended, where people were asked to rate unknown dishes, these items were usually rated higher than quail, trout, and other items normally considered delicacies.

Fruit. There are many wild fruits in the Southeast that are quite tasty, either raw or cooked in pies, cakes, sweetbread, or fermented into wine. Blackberries and, less commonly, dewberries and raspberries, are always favorites. Persimmons are great raw (when they're ripe) or made into sweetbread. Muscadines and fox grapes are good, too, but not as common. I particularly like fox grapes after they've dried on the vine like raisins. Other fruits not quite as common, but quite tasty, are black cherries, wild crabapples, and pawpaws.

Nuts. Most wild nuts are good, such as black walnuts and hickory nuts of several species. But you'd better have a hammer and a big rock to crack them, or teeth stronger than mine. In the river bottoms, wild pecans are quite tasty, and if you're lucky you can find hazelnuts growing wild. Acorns are a good carbohydrate source, but tannic acid makes them bitter—red oak more so than white oak. Native Americans leached the acid out by soaking the acorn "meats" in water, then ground them into flour to make bread. Beech nuts fit this category, too.

Greens. In the spring and early summer, succulent greens are quite good. Raw watercress, found in freshwater streams and springs, is delicious, especially covered with hot oil and vinegar dressing, with a little salt and pepper. Pokeweed leaves, or "poke salat" is good when boiled, but only when the shoots are young and tender, early in the spring. Dandelion leaves are good too, as a fresh salad. Ramps, a type of wild onion, are good in the spring, but you don't want to eat them just before a date. One of my favorite meals is fresh mountain trout, cooked in margarine right on the stream bank, and served with a side of fresh, raw ramps.

Tubers/roots. There are a lot of edible roots and tubers, but the one I've had some experience with is cattail roots, which can be peeled and boiled in water. This one needs some salt and a little spice (hot sauce is good), or it will have a fairly bland taste.

Mushrooms. I don't have to tell you that you can get into trouble with mushrooms if you don't know what you're doing. The one I know well is the morel, the little wrinkle-top mushroom you can find during turkey season. Washed and cooked with butter, this one will "fling a craving on you."

Lesser-Known Foods. A couple of other things are tasty, easy to gather, but hard to get enough to make a meal. Beggarweed is one—the little triangular seed that sticks to your pants when you're quail hunting. If you break the cover off, the inside tastes like raw peanuts. And the other (it's hard to believe) is cocklebur, which has two small, very tasty seeds inside. In fact, if we could easily process cockleburs, they would probably rival soybeans for taste and utility.

In this modern day, when food is so abundant and inexpensive, wild foods are a topic of only casual interest. But it's comforting to me to know that I could survive on the land if I had to. It's also a novelty to occasionally supplement the everyday "tame" foods with wild morsels. Our family commonly eats venison. And wild turkey at Thanksgiving—well, that's a tradition at our house. My wife is a wonderful wild-game cook, and she expects wild turkey for Thanksgiving. So every spring I dutifully go turkey hunting to keep from disappointing her. It's a tough job, but somebody has to do it!

"Making Do" Off the Land

I grew up in an area known as Pea Ridge. I never did know exactly what that means, but it probably refers to the area's poor clay soil. Back then, folks often used the term "making do." My parents and other adults had lived through the Depression, either as adults or as children. Making do to them meant surviving in hard times. There was no need to complain, because everybody had the same hard time, and there were no welfare lines to stand in. They had to gather all the resources they could, use their heads, and survive—make do.

Making do is almost a lost art today. In these times of megabucks and assembly lines, we tend to overspecialize. To make do, on the other hand, you have to know a little about a lot of different things. You have to have common sense, and you have to be hungry. You have to observe and tune in to what the market needs and what it will pay for. And if you're a landowner, making do often involves using your natural resources.

I was on a farm a few years ago with a couple of foresters and a few landowners. We were exploring ways the landowner could best manage his timber. We were discussing one large mature tree in particular and deciding whether it should be cut down to make room for healthier, younger trees. Someone suggested that it be cut up for firewood. I thought that it looked like basswood and asked a forester. He confirmed that it was. A couple of weeks before, my wife and I had talked to some wood carvers at a craft fair in Gatlinburg. They were telling us how hard it was to find good carving wood. After a little discussion, I found out that one of their favorites is basswood, in two-foot-long chunks, as big in diameter as they could find. Now, this tree was about twenty-two inches DBH (diameter at breast height).

I quickly estimated it was worth maybe three hundred to four hundred dollars. But the tree was only worth that much if the landowner knew it, and was willing to take the trouble to find the right market. Most people who want a specialty product will come get it, if they know it's available.

At the craft fair, my wife and I watched a young man making Christmas wreaths out of a smooth, pliable, easy-to-work vine. He was selling decorated wreaths for fifteen to fifty dollars each. I asked him what kind of vine it was, and how hard it was to grow and gather. He laughed and said that it was kudzu, it was easy to gather, and landowners paid him to get rid of it. My wife and I thought that was pretty neat, so we invaded a couple of kudzu patches around Knoxville. Within thirty minutes, we had all the vines I could get into my pickup. She made and gave away at least a dozen wreaths to several friends during Christmas. A little ribbon here and there, and they looked mighty good.

Until a few years ago, I raised Hampshire and Suffolk sheep. These breeds are known more for their meat than for their wool. The going market rate for wool in those days was forty-five to seventy cents per pound at the wool auction. My wife knew some spinners who were excited when they found out we had wool for sale. They had been paying six to twelve dollars a pound. Of course, what they had been buying was clean and long and in better condition than the wool we sold at auction. I asked a few of them how they would like for me to care for the wool in order for them to be interested. They told me to grow it a little longer than most shepherds do, wash the sheep about two weeks before shearing (to allow time for the lanolin to be replaced), shear the fleece in one piece, roll it into a bundle, and tie it with cotton twine. They said if I'd do this, they'd pay me four dollars a pound. Another thing that caught my eye was that sheep manure was selling by the bag in lawn-and-garden centers—and for a pretty hefty price, too. I had a barn full! It obviously had to be collected, dried, bagged, and marketed. But for enough money, that's no problem.

When I was a boy, I sold eastern red cedar Christmas trees. They didn't cost anything to grow. In fact, they grew in spite of us. I simply cut the good ones, piled them on the back of my dad's '51 Chevy pickup and turned them into cash before Christmas at the courthouse square. I used to gather hickory nuts and walnuts and sell them during the fall. Mistletoe, gathered on hunting trips, sold for twenty-five cents a sprig when I was a lad. And most of the city folks didn't even know where it grew. Making Christmas wreaths from pine boughs and florist wire used to be a favorite. By attaching three or four pine cones at the bottom, this was decoration enough.

I like to gather ginseng during the early bow-hunting season, when the leaves are yellow and the red berries are visible. I always plant seeds in the spots where I gather roots. Most people know ginseng is worth a lot of money. But not many folks know that you can sell several kinds of roots and herbs off your land. In fact, there's a place in Carter County, Tennessee, that buys up to thirty-five different items, ranging (in alphabetical order) from angelica root to witch hazel leaves.

Other items from the land are valuable, too—furs, for example. As a matter of fact, the hospital and doctor bills when my daughter was born were paid from furs I caught in my spare time that winter.

I once ran across an article that discussed the value of meteorite pieces that may be lying around on some farmers' land. According to the article, the best way to tell if that unusual-looking rock is a meteorite is to break off a corner and file it to see if there are any shiny particles.

If you're a landowner, it's likely you have several natural resources on your land you can cash in on. Admittedly, gathering the products, and making that market connection, is sometimes tough. But with a little advertising, people will often come to you. I wouldn't be surprised if you couldn't get your barn cleaned out if you simply put an ad in the paper to tell home gardeners that you have this valuable manure you would sell at a reasonable price.... Who knows? It's worth a try.

Spending Time Outdoors

When I was a child, I promised myself I would follow a career path that would allow me to spend time outdoors. I more or less kept that promise, even though now I find myself indoors more than I would like. But I still make time to get outdoors on a regular basis—even though I often have to go against the grain of society's expectations. Being outdoors is like a tonic that I take regularly to keep stress at bay. Outside, I find a predictable order to things. Outside, I can put life's cares in their proper perspective.

The Silent Hills

I sit and watch the silent hills shimmer in gold and green in the Rocky Mountain breeze. And the peace is rare and fine. Oh, God, what a majestic view. The grandeur overwhelms me. I can only tarry a moment, though; I have things to do and places to go. Important, yes, but only because I have made them so in my mind. What's really important is clearing my head—here—now. This peace I feel is so long overdue. How wonderful! And as I sit and watch, the seasons change before my eyes, at least in my mind. The black clouds gather and the wind picks up. The golden leaves go crazy, and the rain and thunder wash me in the swirling masses of the clouds. But still I sit, cleansed and triumphant. I am the only one to have felt this—I've shared this with God. He speaks to me in his wonders—and I understand.

Being outdoors is like a tonic I take regularly to keep stress at bay. Here I find a predictable order to things. Here I can put life's cares in their proper perspective. This old stump collects moisture, which speeds its decay and that of other cast forest material. Soon they'll convert to organic matter and nutrients to feed future trees.

The wind subsides and trees drip. The sun comes out. The birds sing and ground squirrels scurry, stopping now and then to shake the rain from their fur. The sun soon dries the living wonders of this place.

And in a wink, the golden aspen leaves fall—as do the snowflakes, one by one, so dainty, so light, so perfect and beautiful. And I remain, staring in wonder at the silent hills, until mantled in quietness, in white splendor and breathtaking beauty, they soothe my tired soul. My emotions soar, and the wetness in my eyes is all right, since no one sees. It's good. They would not understand. For inside, my heart aches for this serenity. These silent hills are my peace, my strength, and my comfort. They call me and I must go. And here I am in my mind.

And though the winter is hard, I remain. From the cold and suffering come strength and a knowing that here is real life—life in its fullest. I am warmed by a flickering campfire, somewhere in my memory—on a cold, still, star-filled night. While the smoke lazily wafts starward, the new snow sparkles in a million facets of splendor.

The snow melts and I remain. Wizened now. Callused and toughened, I feel the earth stir beneath me as I watch the silent hills. Slowly at first, but soon at a frenzied pace, the ground, the earth, the hills, and the sky come alive. The birds and squirrels now have new meaning to their chatter.

Somehow the newness too soon fades. The leaves toughen to a leathered green, the insects drone, and the sweat on my neck makes me lean back into the blackened shade, which moves as I sleep. But the silent hills never leave my mind. And they never will. Thank you, Lord.

Feeling at Home Outdoors

I'm told that most accidents happen in the home, yet home is where folks feel the most comfortable. That's where we go to relax, kick our shoes off, and take naps—we feel protected there. Away from home we have to maintain a certain vigilance, keep up our guard.

I've always felt pretty much at home in the outdoors. I feel relaxed there, I feel comfortable there, I can kick off my shoes if I want to—and, yes, even take naps now and then. I've always taken this for granted. I grew up in the country, where I spent a great deal of time outdoors. As an adult I still spend all the time I can there.

But I've come to realize that most folks these days don't feel comfortable outdoors at all. They're scared of discomfort, injury, or even death. These same folks don't wince about getting into a twenty-five-hundred-pound death machine and driving along a packed freeway at seventy miles an hour, and maybe they drive to a community of a million people, some of whom steal, rape, and kill—and who can't easily be identified from all the others. Why the difference?

After quite some thought, I believe the answer lies in familiarity. Most systems—natural or artificial—have an order. And until we become familiar with the system, we don't understand the order. Until we understand the order, we're not comfortable. We know the danger of a car and take precautions to minimize the danger; the same goes for driving in traffic. In most cases we know how to avoid the people who would cause us harm, and where to go for help if we need it. We know the system has a safety net (police, hospitals, etc.) and how to quickly access it. We're familiar with the order of the system. There's order to the natural system that operates outdoors, too. It's just that, unfortunately, not many folks today are familiar enough with it.

I've spent a great deal of time trying to help folks, particularly youngsters, become familiar with the natural order. I want them to feel comfortable outdoors—to enjoy it as much as I do. If young folks don't grow up appreciating and liking the outdoors, we're in trouble.

So, I start by identifying all the things they can think of that can hurt them, kill them, or at least make them feel uncomfortable outside. Over the years, here's how the list goes:

Suckers, Biters, and Stingers
ticks and chiggers
deer flies, mosquitoes, no-see-ums
bees, wasps, and hornets
snakes
spiders
Poison Plants
poison ivy and poison oak
poison sumac
mushrooms
Harsh Weather
cold
hot
wet
sunburn
Hunger and Thirst
Getting Lost
Large Predators

That's about it. Occasionally someone mentions ghosts, but they usually feel better when I tell them that even if ghosts were there, ghosts can go anywhere. So the outdoors is no more dangerous in terms of ghosts than anywhere else. Now, the way we deal with dangerous or uncomfortable elements of our human-made world is to learn how to identify them and how to protect ourselves from them or avoid them. The same goes for the natural world. Let's take the suckers, biters, and stingers, for example. The first thing is to break them down into groups. For ticks and chiggers, the easiest way to protect yourself is to spray critical areas of your clothing with a product containing Permethrin or Deet (N, N-diethyl-m-toluamide) (see the piece entitled "About Ticks" in the "Summer" chapter below). Mosquitoes, deer flies, and no-see-ums can be repelled with Deet applied to vulnerable skin areas. The best thing to do against stingers is to be careful. Don't swat or irritate them, stay away from their nests, and if you're stung put chewing tobacco, baking soda, or a slice of white potato on the area. These draw the venom out of the wound. If you're allergic to stings, keep appropriate medicine with you. With snakes, learn to identify the rattlesnakes, copperheads, cottonmouths, and coral snakes. All the rest in North America are completely harmless. Be careful around the venomous ones, and if you're bitten, remember—national statistics reveal that 99.8 percent of the victims recover. If you're within an hour of a doctor, don't treat the bite at all: go straight to the doctor. If you're more than an hour from a doctor, carry a snake-bite kit along. Among spiders, only two—the black widow and the brown recluse—can cause us problems. And more people are bitten by these around the house than in the outdoors. Be careful around those two. If you're bitten, place a white potato half over the bite and go to the doctor. If you're allergic to poison ivy, poison oak, or poison sumac, learn to identify them and try not to let the sap of the leaves, vines, or roots touch you. Also, don't burn vines unless you know what kind they are. If you get the rash, use calamine lotion to stop the itching. If you don't know which mushrooms to eat, it's simple: don't eat mushrooms! Almost anybody can recognize the wrinkled morel though, and it's too good a morsel to pass up. To stay warm or cool, dress in layers (see my essay entitled "Dressing Smart Helps Whip Winter Winds" near the end of Part II). To stay dry in damp weather, use a Gore-Tex garment. But in downpours you will need a heavy vinyl rainsuit with welded seams. If you sunburn easily, use sunscreen or cover your skin with a light cotton shirt and wear a wide-brim hat. I never go outdoors for any period of time without some food and water. Nut and raisin mixes are a high-energy food. You can carry the mix conveniently in a Ziploc bag and water in an empty twenty-ounce plastic soft drink bottle (it makes an excellent canteen). To keep from getting lost, carry a compass. Take a reading before you start out and tie a road, stream, or other land form to a compass bearing.

It's amazing to me how many people are afraid of large animals. Let's review all the large animals in North America that are potentially harmful: polar bears, grizzly bears, black bears, alligators, and mountain lions. Well, most of us don't live around these anyway. But if you do, the thing to keep in mind is that they don't normally eat people. In fact, they're usually *scared* of people! If you do come into contact with them, stay calm and don't run if charged. Pepper spray should be a constant companion if you're hunting in grizzly country. And the main thing: *don't corner one*!

That's it. For all practical purposes, these are about all the things that can cause us problems in the outdoors. And there's something we can do to prevent or remedy every one of them.

Now for those of you afraid to be indoors. First we'll need to list all the things that can cause you problems. Let's see—the iron, the stove, the electric outlets....

Wild Enough for Bobcats

When my business day becomes especially hectic, I crave an escape to the wild. Or if my day is routine and boring (it seldom is), I daydream about raw adventure in the outdoors. In these mind escapes, I search for wild things in wild places.

What are wild things in wild places? Well, it depends on perspective. To some, the city park with its peanut-hungry squirrels and pigeons is wild enough. To others, a simple ten-acre woodlot with its resident bluejays and towhees is a wild place. The fact is, when I was a kid just such a place was my wilderness. My adventures there were just as exciting as those of Tarzan in his magnificent jungle.

As I analyze it now, I think it was the degree to which animals, plants, and life processes were unknown that made the place seem wild to me. As my horizon grew with education and I came to understand my little woodlot better, the wild became more tame. And as my footsteps grew farther apart, the vastness became smaller. The expansive jungle became a mere ten-acre woodlot.

Incidentally, I visited my jungle recently and found its magnificent variety of life reduced to little more than a lounging spot for cattle. Destruction of the forest duff and soil compaction by thousands of cattle footprints had changed the little stream from a babbling brook with shady holes and glittering darters to a brown sewer. My jungle once held a new adventure around every curve of its green, serpentine path, but now I can stand on one side and see the pasture on the other. It saddens me as I wonder if a spot so tame would ever seem wild to today's children. Would it stir the pulse, pump the adrenaline, or inspire creativity?

Today, a wild place to me is where I can walk all day without crossing a road or seeing another soul. Not many places like that are left in this country, except our national parks. Don't misunderstand though. It doesn't take a place that wild for me to enjoy the out-of-doors. I enjoy an outing—even a stroll through the city park. But for me to enjoy it to the fullest, I prefer a place wild enough for bobcats.

Deer are wild, but they'll chew their cud in a subdivision if folks aren't looking. Even wild turkeys, once thought to be denizens of the deep, dark forest are now known to come up to barns and peck right along with the chickens. But tell me, have you ever known a bobcat to voluntarily take up around folks? It's hard to tame the wild streak out of them, even when they're forced into captivity.

Bobcats conjure up images of wildness in just about all folks. A farmer recently was describing a couple of tracts of land where I could hunt. He said, "Now you can hunt either place. They both have deer, lots of 'em, but the river bottom down there—now that place is sure 'nuff wild. You're likely to find anything down there—it even has bobcats!"

Bobcats are so elusive and shy that few people have ever seen one, and they are believed by many to be endangered. Actually, they are fairly widespread throughout North America where sufficient forested habitat is still available. It's the only "wild" cat found throughout most of its range, particularly the Southeast. Except for parts of Florida, the larger cougar has been virtually eliminated from the southeastern states. Other than being smaller, the bobcat has a short tail, distinguishing it from the cougar, which has a long tail. Bobcats range from twelve to thirty pounds, and its color ranges from yellowish brown to gray with numerous black or brown spots and streaks. They have a varied diet, but rabbits are a major staple.

In the 1970s, the U.S. Endangered Species Act reduced the use of endangered spotted cat furs from South America, Asia, and Africa. Trappers and furriers responded by turning to the bobcat as a substitute—and the annual harvest rose to about 90,000. Before 1970, a pelt from Maine, for example, was worth about $4, but by the late 1970s it had jumped to $55. In a few cases, fur dealers paid up to $150 for a prime Maine pelt.

All this activity caused concern in the wildlife conservation community about the bobcat's status. In response, Congress in 1982 required the U.S. Fish and Wildlife Service to monitor population levels and the annual harvest. Prior to 1970, we didn't know much about bobcats. Now there has been a great deal of research done on the species, and we know more about its status. In New Jersey, wild-caught bobcats were successfully relocated to areas where populations had been depleted. I'm glad. I hope that someday my great-grandson can find a place wild enough for bobcats. I hope he can call up an old tom bobcat while he's turkey hunting and feel a chill of excitement up his spine—just like I have!

River Adventure

My first extended river float was a happening. My friend Don and I were wildlife graduate students with the spring quarter blues. Research paper deadlines and exam cramming were taking their toll, when late one night during a coffee break from studying, we hit upon a terrific idea. The minute our exams were over, we'd head out on a river float adventure. Over the next few weeks, we pored over maps until we found the perfect place—a fifty-mile stretch of the Tallapoosa River in north Alabama, with only one road across it. From that point on we didn't do a lot of planning, but we sure did a lot of daydreaming.

Sure enough, the minute exams were over, we rushed home and crammed a few things in a rucksack. I loaded my twelve-foot johnboat in the back of my '65 Ford pickup and threw in a sleeping bag, army cot, Coleman stove, and lantern. We'd decided to buy groceries on the way, but I did throw in a little flour and salt and some dried white beans—they just happened to be handy. I grabbed a fishing pole, and at the last minute decided to throw in my .22 rifle. Little did I know at the time how good that decision was!

I jumped in the truck, picked up Don, and we hit the road. We stopped on the way and bought several sacks of groceries, enough for five days, and put them on top of the other gear, which was already loaded in the boat in the back of the truck. Boy, were we excited! We were finally on our way—five glorious days in the outdoors, away from exams, civilization, and, most of all, professors. We picked up one of Don's friends along the way who was supposed to drop us off and pick us up five days and fifty miles later.

The road into the drop-off point was long, dusty, and bumpy—in fact, it was full of big rocks and holes. We bounced so high our heads hit the ceiling of the cab—we were sure glad to get there. We jerked the loaded boat out of the truck, slid it into the water, and waved goodbye to Don's friend as we shoved off. As the truck bounced out of sight, and the sound of the engine faded, all we could hear was the sound of water gently sliding over algae-covered boulders. Soon we heard rushing water. A glance ahead made us sit up and take notice. All we could see was whitewater slapping at boulders. We braced ourselves for the thrill. Four minutes, three scrapes, and two bumps later, we emerged into a near placid, but gently flowing pool. How good it was to be alive!

The river turned out to be excellent, with exciting rapids alternating with long slow pools. Pretty soon, we were navigating like pros. I would guide us from the front with the short paddle, and Don, who dwarfed me by six inches and fifty pounds, provided the long-paddled power stroke when needed.

After a couple of hours we got hungry. We were in for a shock: no groceries! They had apparently bounced out of the truck on the bumpy road. I'd always heard this stuff about surviving off the land, but I'd never had to try it. As we were reviewing our options, I remembered the dried white beans I'd packed before leaving home. I frantically dug through the gear. There they were—great! I dipped a potful of water out of the river, cranked up the Coleman stove, poured in the beans, and let them boil as we continued down the river. (Nobody had ever told me they needed to soak overnight first.) After about thirty minutes, Don asked, "Them beans ready yet?" We were both pretty hungry by that time. The first crunch told us something was definitely wrong. We boiled them for thirty more minutes; by this time we were starving. Crunchy or not, we ate all we could stand. We reviewed our options again. Muskrats were everywhere, and I remembered my rifle. You talk about a humbling experience for a west Tennessee squirrel hunter! After fifteen shots at river rats swimming in zig-zag fashion across the river at five miles an hour while we traveled downriver at the same speed, I finally hit one. My biggest problem was that Don was laughing so hard the boat was rocking.

For supper that night we had roasted muskrat and semihard beans—not bad. For breakfast we had roasted muskrat and good beans. For lunch we had cold roasted muskrats and no beans. Ditto for supper. Needless to say, by the middle of the third day, when we finally came to a bridge, we were ready for civilized food. After a two-mile hike, we found a little store and were back in business.

The trip was great. Between rapids, we'd lay back, relax, and talk about how few people knew about such pleasures—and how if more did, it wouldn't be as enjoyable because the river would be crowded. Sometimes we'd just jump overboard in our cut-off jeans to get cool, swim around a little, get back in the boat, and sun dry.

One evening about sundown we pulled into a little cove to camp for the night. We set out a few fishing lines, pitched camp, cooked us up a good meal, and told stories around the campfire under a star-studded sky. Life truly couldn't be better than this. When we got so sleepy our stories weren't making sense anymore, we crawled into our bags and drifted off to sleep to the crackling of the fire and soft murmur of the river.

The next thing I knew, I was being rudely awakened by Don frantically shaking me and hollering, "Wake up Jim, we've got a fire." As I opened my eyes, it looked like the whole world was ablaze. We jumped up, grabbed a quilt apiece, and headed for the water. With our wet quilts we quickly beat out the fire, which had apparently started from a hot coal that had rolled out to some dry leaves. Luckily, only a few square yards of woods burned, but I sure learned a valuable lesson about campfire safety that night.

We saw only one person during the whole five days. An old fisherman was dunking nightcrawlers in a curve of the river as we drifted into view. I guess he hadn't seen many sights like us before, maybe never. After squinting to size us up, he finally spat and asked, "Where you boys goin'?" We told him we were going to the next highway. His eyes widened and he shook his head. "Reckon you'll be goin' through Devil Shoals then—be careful." His stare returned to his bobber as we drifted on by. Needless to say, Don and I didn't exactly look forward to what lay ahead. It must have been about three hours later when we heard a roar that more nearly resembled a tornado than a river shoals. As we got closer we could barely hear each other as we compared options. Before we knew it, we were already committed.

To make a long story short, we survived—even without turning over. But I'm here to tell you: there's never been a carnival ride even close to the thrill we experienced that afternoon at Devil Shoals. In a few more miles we reached our destination, totally relaxed, at peace with the world, and a little sad it was over. The trip only lasted five days, but the memories of it will be with me until I close my eyes for good—and the memories seem to get more vivid every year.

A Compass and a Little Common Sense

"Where's that doggoned bank?" The tone of Dad's voice confirmed the doubt I was beginning to feel. "I believe it's over to the right," my father-in-law ventured. I managed to wait a full thirty seconds before giving my opinion. "Nope, I think it's to the left." As the three of us in Dad's fourteen-foot Alumna-Craft idled around and around in the pea-soup fog, I had to chuckle to myself. There we were, where Cypress Creek entered the Tennessee River—an area the three of us knew like the back of our hands—yet we were completely turned around (that's a term we accomplished woodsmen use when we don't want to admit we're lost). It was predawn on the first day of the 1990 squirrel season, and light was coming fast. After wandering around for at least twenty minutes, I finally asked, "Do either of you have a compass?" "Yep," Dad replied. After opening it up, I couldn't believe my eyes. We were going 180 degrees from where it seemed we ought to be. We finally got straightened out, I found the bank, and we arrived at the hunting site thirty minutes late.

Compasses don't lie. At least good ones don't. I spent nearly forty years of my life without knowing that—I mean *really* knowing that. As I sit here in the Chicago airport writing, I chuckle once again at a question I was once asked by a newspaper columnist. "Have you ever been lost?" he asked, with a straight face. Well, no self-respecting woodsman is ever going to admit he was lost! That's what happens to little old ladies and desk jockeys. But, unfortunately, Mom taught me to always be honest. I thought for a minute—just how should I pose my answer? I knew my hunting prowess and credibility as a woodsman were on the line—I also knew my mom was watching.

Fact is, I've never been lost for a long period of time, but I have been completely turned around for an hour or two (I still find it hard to say lost). On one occasion, when I was doing my doctoral research on deer, I was so disoriented (another safe term), the only direction I knew for sure was down. And that was only because I had the ground under my feet, and the ground is down. I was capturing deer with a dart gun at 2:00 A.M. in a 250-square-mile floodplain of the Tensaw River in south Alabama. After darting a deer, it wandered in circles for some distance from the Jeep before going down. I instrumented her with a radio transmitter and waited until she recovered. After she ran off, I started back to the old army Jeep. Then it occurred to me—I had no idea which direction it was! I walked around and around for about twenty minutes, when it further dawned on me that 250 square miles is a lot of bottomland, and I could be getting farther away instead of closer. I was tired anyway, so I lay down and went to sleep on the leaf-littered, cracked-mud floor. As dawn broke, I stood up and looked around. There, not over forty yards away, was the Jeep. I went straight to a hardware store and bought some reflective tape for the old Jeep.

Back to my discovery—that a compass doesn't lie. A few years ago, I was bowhunting for elk and deer with two friends in the Colorado mountains, at an elevation of about 10,000 feet. Our hunting area was about 2 miles from camp, at a drop in elevation of some 700 feet. Ken had taken a fat mule deer that morning, so Mike and I helped him drag it the grueling 2 miles back up the mountain to camp. After lunch Mike and I headed down the mountain while Ken took his deer the 42 miles back to town for processing. As we separated to go to our evening stands, we agreed to meet at a small pond just after dark.

Needless to say, when we met that evening, Mike and I were both tired, and hungry enough to eat a road-killed 'possum. Then I had this bright idea. "Mike," I said, "let's try a shortcut. The old logging trail is the long way. If we go straight through the black timber, we'll probably save half a mile, maybe more. I've never been that way, but it should be easy. Once we hit the bluff, we'll just head left, right into camp." "Okay," Mike said, "whatever you think." I confidently struck out through the black timber, with Mike right behind me.

The person who coined the term "black timber" must have tried to find his way through a several-thousand-acre chunk of it at night. The coniferous canopy is so dense you can't see the stars. And trees don't seem to rot out west (I guess there's not enough moisture); they just seem to lie there forever, by the thousands, getting in the way. You can't go through them, and by the time you've gone around a few dozen of them at night, your sense of direction is shot. After we'd gone far enough to have hit the bluff but hadn't, I decided to resort to the compass. It wasn't working. It said we were going east, when we were really going west. I shook it. No good. I rapped it against a tree trunk. No good. Mike tapped me on the shoulder and said, "Jim, compasses don't lie." It went against all my instincts, but I turned around and headed west according to the compass, then put it in my pocket. After we had walked around downed trees for another forty-five minutes, I got the compass out again. Same deal! I turned around again and put the compass back in my pocket. This time I checked the compass after about thirty minutes. I couldn't believe it. We were going east again! This time I took the compass out and held it where I could constantly see it until we reached the bluff. When we arrived at camp, we found that Ken had dozed off to sleep with spaghetti simmering on the stove. It was now a dry clump with all the properties of a rubber ball. I cut it in two with my hunting knife, and we gnawed on it until we fell asleep.

I've come to a conclusion. Anyone who tells you he hasn't been lost, either hasn't spent much time outdoors, or—well, I wouldn't trust him with a worn-out Bible. But with a compass and a little common sense, anyone can figure their way out—as long as they believe their compass.

Owning a Four-Wheel-Drive

Well, I finally did it. After thirty years of getting stuck, walking two miles to my treestand, and then dragging my deer out of the woods that far, and sometimes farther, I finally bought a four-wheel-drive pickup. Not only had

I never owned a four-wheel-drive, I'd never paid over $4,500 for a truck. It's true, hard to believe, but true—and I've owned a truck continuously since 1965. What's more, before 1989, I'd never owned one with air-conditioning, power windows, power door locks, power steering, steering-wheel tilt, etc. In fact, all five of my trucks before this one had been stripped-down custom models. And all but two had been used when I bought them. (Come to think of it, I guess that's why I'd never paid more than $4,500.) I tend to drive my old trucks until just before the wheels fall off. One of the best trucks I ever owned was a '79 Ford. It had 162,000 trouble-free miles on it, when one morning, I woke up to discover it was gone—it had been stolen!

The previous day, I had been bowhunting for deer, and after being soaked by an unexpected rain which set in for the night, I decided to roll up my sleeping bag and head for a nearby motel to dry out. Besides, I reasoned, after two days of sweating, I needed a shower anyway. I was ready to head out before daylight next morning when I realized my truck was not where I thought I parked it. I walked around the motel and realized it was indeed gone. I thought I'd lost my mind! Who would steal a '79 pickup with 162,000 miles on it when new vehicles were parked all around? (Smart thieves—they knew a good truck when they saw one.) The police found it a week later, stripped and rolled off the side of a mountain. Incidentally, I had taken my bow into the motel that night, so I called a wildlife officer friend, Steve Nifong, who took me to my hunting area and left me, then picked me up that night. I took a nice fat doe that day.

Back to four-wheel-drives. I drove a four-wheel-drive for a few months when I was conducting deer research with the Auburn University Cooperative Wildlife Research Unit. It was an old Willy's Jeep, World War II vintage, that was tough as nails but looked like it had gone through both world wars. I got it stuck twice, once in log skidder ruts and once on a tree stump. By the time I got it out of the skidder tracks, I had to open the doors so that water (steering wheel deep) could drain out. It sure was convenient, though, and for the next twenty-two years I wanted a four-wheel-drive, but didn't want to spend that much money.

When I finally went shopping for one, I had a lot to learn. Now, you can buy four-wheel-drive cars, family wagons, play vehicles, and pickup trucks. There are little trucks, mid-size trucks, and full-size pickups. There are regular cabs, big cabs, and crew cabs (with four doors); there are trucks with long wheelbases and short wheelbases. You can buy automatic-locking front hubs or manual-locking hubs. Apparently, besides the convenience of not having to get out to lock the automatic hubs, there is no other advantage. The disadvantage with the automatic-locking hubs seems to be that the front axles rotate all the time, whether the four-wheel-drive gear is engaged or not, and this causes them to wear faster. Four-wheel-drives usually come standard with a heavier suspension system than two-wheel-drives, and you can buy an even heavier suspension package as an option. Another option you can get is a limited slip (or "posi-traction") axle, in the rear or the front. It seems that a standard two-wheel-drive is really only a one-wheel-drive; that is, there's power only in one wheel. A four-wheel-drive without limited slip is really a two-wheel-drive, with power to one back wheel and to one front wheel. Limited slip in the rear gives power to three wheels, and you don't really have power to all four wheels unless you have a four-wheel-drive with limited slip on both rear and front. Maybe everybody else knew all that but me.

When I went shopping I planned to buy a stripped-down custom four-wheel-drive, with no fancy stuff. But because the dealership was overstocked with straight shifts and it was trying to clear the lot to make room for the newest models, I got an offer I couldn't refuse. The difference in cost between a stripped-down model and one with all the luxuries—power everything, air, tilt, cruise, carpet, extra handling package, radial all-season tires, fancy light package, stereo, trim, etc.—was only $750. Since I was going all the way, I also picked one with limited-slip in the rear (another $300). So, in 1989, I bought a four-wheel-drive Cadillac with a Ford emblem and three wheels that pulled. Sounds strange to me, even now. If some of you farmers and ranchers out there think I sound naive, I am—or at least I was.

I've noticed four-wheel-drive owners over the years. Some are farmers, surveyors, and others who use them as a professional tool. Some use them to hunt and fish with in out-of-the-way places. Some use them to play with, running up and down muddy roads, muddy hills, and sandy beaches, often tearing up the terrain by causing it to erode. Some hunters and fishermen are careless, too, tearing up logging roads and farmers' fields. And some own four-wheel-drives so they can put oversized tires on and drive around town to impress folks. Oh, yes, and some put super-sized tires on and run over junk cars for a living. Whatever. I've made myself a promise, though. I plan to respect the land. Like a gun, it's not the instrument that's the problem—it's the one who uses it.

Part II

Seasons

Spring

One of the things I love about Tennessee is that there are four distinct seasons, which is not so in some places. Some places around the equator have only one, and in other places, there are two at most. Spring and fall get pretty much left out in south Alabama, for example.

Spring is always special. As the earth gets closer to the sun, the warming soil soon comes alive with new energy. Increasing day length stirs hormones and emotion, soon erupting into sound, bright colors, and activity.

Turkey Behavior Signals Spring

It all starts in the spring. Sometimes I think God had turkeys and turkey hunters in mind when he invented spring. As the days lengthen, things begin to happen in the turkey world. It's about the same time that dogwood buds swell and cardinals slowly begin to come out of their winter silence with a sluggish "wha-cheer, wha-cheer." Cricket frogs limber up at the roadside seeps, and spring peepers sing their evening symphony. Flocks of bachelor turkey gobblers begin to break up about this time, as their gonads swell, producing testosterone which triggers other hormones in the body. Strange things begin to happen, not only in the turkey's body, but in his mind as well. He begins to walk a little prouder, a little straighter, and strut his stuff a little more. The gobbler that has largely been silent all winter, except for an occasional "putt," now begins to gobble early in the morning. To the

Spring is always special. As the earth gets closer to the sun, the warming soil soon comes alive with new energy. A single buttercup at an old house site.

birdwatcher, the gobble is a tribute to spring; to the turkey it's serious business, but it's music to a turkey hunter's ears. Gobbling usually lasts until about mid-morning, but as the mating season goes on, turkeys will occasionally gobble later in the day.

In the turkey world, gobblers quickly establish a pecking order, and hens do, too. Gobblers seldom fight, because it's not necessary. The boss gobbler is pretty well known among the other gobblers. They also know the second in command, the third, and so on. I once saw two old gobblers fight though, down in the Mississippi River bottoms, settling once and for all the question of who was boss (see the piece entitled "One of Nature's Spectacles" in the "Tales about Birds" chapter below). I also watched two Nebraska gobblers "settle the score" one spring.

The turkey hen's response to the gobbler's gobbling, strutting, and otherwise lewd behavior begins with a series of lovesick yelps, usually a series of three. But if a hen is particularly ready for mating she may yelp several times in succession. She may even get excited enough to cackle. A typical cackle is three or four yelps, three or four yelps in fast sequence at a high pitch, and ending with three or four more regularly spaced yelps. Now, the way it works in the turkey world usually is that the turkey gobbler gobbles and hens flock to him to watch him strut. He puffs himself into a ball, fans his tail feathers, drops his wing tips to the ground, and takes a series of short, choppy steps with his head pulled back, his eyes half-closed in ecstasy, and his chest out. After a brief display, the gobbler mounts the hen, and a short period of mating takes place. Dave Smith, a good friend of mine who studied turkey behavior in Texas, has a hunch that the dangling beard of the turkey gobbler in front of the hen's face keeps her mesmerized until mating is over. Only the mature turkey gobbler has a beard long enough for this. Turkey gobblers that are only a year old (called "jakes") have a beard usually no longer than three or four inches. One turkey gobbler may accumulate a harem of from half a dozen to a dozen or more hens. They will stay with him early in the morning, and then by mid-morning, one by one, they begin to peel off, eventually leaving the gobbler by himself. They steal away to secretive places to nest. This happens every day until ten or eleven eggs are laid and the nest is complete.

For the next twenty-eight days, the hen spends a lot of time on the nest incubating the eggs. Eventually, if all goes well and the eggs have not been disturbed by predators (such as skunks, raccoons, or snakes), the eggs hatch into little balls of multicolored fuzz about the size of a baby chick. Young turkeys are ready to go almost as soon as they are hatched, following their mother around from place to place. When predators approach, such as hawks overhead, the little turkeys "freeze" in nearly perfect camouflage against the leaves in the woods.

It's about time—just a few more weeks now. I can almost hear the old boy gobbling on the other ridge—and the ten o'clock sun sure feels good on my back. I can't wait.

Turkey Hunting Camp

You know, one of the greatest benefits I glean from hunting is the peace and solitude I find outdoors. I remember times when I would go hunting and not see another soul for five or six days—now that's solitude. In fact, when I was doing graduate research, I would spend three months at a time when I would see people only once a week. I don't do that much anymore. Oh, I still find solitude—on a regular basis—but in smaller intervals. These days I seldom hunt and camp by myself for more than two or three days at a time.

A hunting camp provides the best of both worlds. During the day while you're hunting by yourself, you have peace and solitude. In the early morning and evening, you share meals, fellowship, and hunting stories with friends.

Let me tell you about one of the really good hunting camps—one that builds memories and bonds friendships. It's a turkey-hunting camp in Missouri that a group of fellows and I joined about 1984. And though we've added a few hunters over the years, and a few have quit coming, there's a central core of folks that keeps the tradition going.

There's nothing special about the facilities, just a little clearing next to a gravel road way back in the middle of the Mark Twain National Forest. That's it. No tables, running water, or garbage cans—just a clearing. In fact, the clearing is not much of a clearing. As we pitch our tents and park our travel trailers, we have to weave and dodge among the trees. But, as strange as it may sound, I'm glad we don't have facilities—I lean toward undeveloped campgrounds. Now, don't get me wrong—I didn't say some of us don't have conveniences. Far from it. In fact, a couple of folks bring motor homes, with everything in them except automatic tellers.

But it's the people that make a hunting camp, and this one is blessed with some of the best—and some of the most colorful. It also has some of the best hunters I know, but that's not important to camp quality. The number of people varies from year to year and day to day, but there's usually ten to fifteen. Until his death a few years ago, Mr. G was the focal point of the camp. He always arrived a couple of days before the season opened, set up camp, and he'd be there for the duration (turkey season is two weeks long in Missouri). He said his girlfriend didn't like it much, but she just had to live with it. Mr. G in his seventies could walk the socks off the typical teenager. He knew where all the "honey holes" were, and would tell you about them only if you were a newcomer, or if you were down on your turkey-hunting luck—but you had to be *way down*. He didn't have much patience with foul language either. One year, he told a camp visitor from Pennsylvania to clean up his language or leave. The visitor cleaned up his language. Not only that, but he came back almost every evening.

Another interesting camp character was Mr. Billy, an excellent turkey hunter, who had more experience than several of us combined. I don't know how old he was when he passed away, but he began turkey hunting in 1951. Nobody in Tennessee hunted turkeys much back then, so he went down to Alabama to learn from an old turkey hunter, who, as he put it, had "strings of beards crisscrossing his living room several times." Always the gentleman, Mr. Billy wore a necktie with his wool plaid shirt while he was hunting, and in camp. When he was hunting, the collar was buttoned, but he unbuttoned it while relaxing back at camp. His philosophy was that the turkey is a noble creature and deserves our respect. And a good turkey-hunting day to him was one where he could hear a gobble or two and not see too many "pilgrims" (other turkey hunters, to those of you not yet initiated). It was a really good day to him if he could "work a bird" (call and get a gobbler to respond), and the ultimate, of course, was to harvest a gobbler.

I could write a story about every hunter in camp—each one is that interesting. Dr. W is a doctor in Jackson, Tennessee, with as much dry wit as turkey-hunting skill. There are Tommy and Robert, Mr. G's sons, Mike, Dan, Jim J., Fred, Greg, Tony and his son Doug, Phillip, Chuck and his dad, and my long-time friend Billy.

You might imagine that we hear and tell a lot of turkey-hunting stories during the week. We see a lot more gobblers in visions around the campfire than we see in the woods or in the hunter's bag. It's an occasion to learn, too. Hunters especially perk up their ears when a perennially successful hunter tells his tale. There are educational turkey-hunting stories, entertaining stories, exciting stories, and ones with a moral—and then there are the weird ones—you know, the kind that make you want to sniff the 7-Up the teller's been drinking.

Chuck took the award in the weird category one year. It seems he was working this bird who wouldn't come to his call, but went to a farmer when he called the cows to feed. But that's not the weird part. As Chuck was calling, a turkey hen came up and sat down about shotgun length from him. After fifteen or twenty minutes when he shifted his position, the hen didn't turn inside out and vanish amidst dust, feathers, and alarm putts. She just sat there and purred. Weird, but still not the weird part. When he got up to move to a new spot to call from, the hen went with him! Now Chuck is a Tennessee wildlife officer, has taken lots of turkeys, and has a great deal of credibility among the folks at camp. So after he told the story, we calmly got up and escorted him to his cot. He was delirious. It happens after you've been chasing spring gobblers for a few days!

Some Turkeys I Have Known

What a morning! Clear skies, crisp 48 degrees, dogwoods full white, irises blooming purple, a cardinal singing, and not one leaf stirring—one of those rare mornings that turkey hunters dream of. A morning when everything goes right. As I'm writing this piece, I'm soaking in the beauty of the spring hardwoods, relaxing against a big red oak on top of a steep ridge in southeast Missouri. The coffee from my thermos feels so good going down. It's still hot, having been made only a couple of hours before. Everything is right with the world, because, you see, I have just harvested my 1988 gobbler. I take another look at the majestic bird, a fine two-year-old specimen of twenty-two pounds with a ten-inch beard. And he didn't come easy. No eastern wild turkey ever does.

The greatest trophies that turkey hunters have are the memories of birds they have encountered over the years. Each tends to take on a different personality, real or imagined. Most get away—a few don't. Mounted specimens fade and deteriorate over the years. Memories, instead, become more vivid.

I remember one from a warm mid-afternoon in Tennessee. The sky was clear, and the wind was blowing hard as I scouted for sign. I had just climbed a steep ridge and stopped to get my breath. Oak leaves were still the size of a squirrel's ear, and visibility was good. I glanced over to the next ridge, and there in plain view, no more than eighty yards away, was a gobbler in full strut. He hadn't noticed me walking in the leaves because of the wind noise and swaying trees. He was out of range, and visibility was too clear to try to get closer, so I sank to my belly and watched. He was making no sound, except the pfft-t-t-t of his wings as he went into a strut, back erect, then into strut again. I strained to see hens but there weren't any. The only sound was the wind and a strange whine—on again, off again. Every time I heard the whine, he popped into a strut. I finally figured it out. Every time the wind would gust, two trees would rub together, causing the whine. He was courting a hickory and a white oak! He finally gave up and strutted off out of sight.

Another time, I had just elicited a gobble on a distant ridge, at eleven o'clock in the morning. I set my hen decoy thirty yards below me and yelped loudly so I could be heard above the wind. Repeated gobbles, closer and closer, told me the bird was coming—fast. At about sixty-five yards below me—thirty-five yards below the decoy—he stopped to strut and display. He was proud, and, after all, he had come several hundred yards. The least the decoy could do was to move a mere thirty-five yards downhill to him. He persisted for forty-five minutes, showing all his best stuff and gobbling fiercely. Finally, he stared at the decoy, cocked his head to one side, then the other, then walked off indignantly. I don't blame him.

A woodpecker drumming just above my head startles me back to the present. The bird at my feet represents a satisfying climax to six mornings of hard hunting, lots of sweat, and several ten-mile days of climbing up and down steep ridges. Some of those miles were spent walking, looking for scarce sign; some miles were covered by frantically racing up and down steep ridges from one distant gobble to another. The previous night, I had slept only two hours, driving from a late-night commitment 175 miles away. I eased into the woods out to a ridge point barely in time to hoot like a barred owl while the turkeys were still on roost. A distant gobble two ridges to my left stirred my blood and sent me racing down, then up, then down, then up. Panting, I hooted again. The only gobble this time was from another bird three ridges to my right. I waited. No gobble on my ridge. I took a deep breath and tore off downhill again. Several minutes later, I carefully picked my way up to a steep ridge to listen again, to make sure which ridge he was on. Just before I reached the crest, I heard it: "Gil-obble-obble-obble!" Close! So close I quickly picked a tree to back up to. I sat down, pulled down my headnet, put on my gloves, and took out my slate. Three quiet clucks was all it took. A triple gobble! He was on his way. Just forty yards away, over the crest out of sight, two gobblers were trying to out-gobble and out-strut each other. Now the bird on the ridge I just left was gobbling—also the distant one I was racing to. Heart pounding, I readied my Mark 5 Browning. Up periscope. One then two heads cleared the crest. Beards wagging, they came quickly to within twenty-three yards. As I shot, one fell and the other flew. 6:25 A.M. Nice bird, real nice bird; what a beautiful morning!

Nature at Night

One of my favorite things to do in late spring is sit outside at night and listen to the night sounds. That's what I'm doing tonight. It's fantastic. While most folks are asleep or watching the miracle tube, there's a whole world of auditory splendor, just outside waiting to be heard. Tonight, from one spot I can hear several critters. Nearby, there's a "jug-a-rum" bullfrog chorus coming from my neighbor's pond (my pond is strangely quiet). There's an occasional "plunk" call from the bronze frog. Off in the distance, I hear trills from the narrow-mouth toad and the Fowler's toad. To the south I hear the excited yipping of a few coyotes, and all around me are calls of whippoorwills. To the east I hear the plaintive "whoo-oo-oo" of the great horned owl and the raucous "who cooks, who cooks, who cooks for you-awlll" of the barred owl.

Most folks wouldn't go outside without a flashlight. Too bad. They're really missing a lot. People's lights have a way of hiding nature's night splendor. Nature has its own light. The moon, stars, and lightning bugs light up the night sufficiently for folks to see, if they've eaten their carrots (carrots contain plenty of vitamin A, which helps night vision). Of course, you have to allow your eyes time to adjust. Given enough time without artificial light, the pupil expands to help the eye take in as much light as possible. Light-sensitive rods on the retina take over to allow vision. Animals more active at night have more rods, so they can see better. Their eyes actually glow in the dark when an artificial light is shined in their direction (deer, cats, raccoons, etc.).

Many folks are afraid of the dark. That's a shame, because there's a whole new beautiful world they'll never experience in artificial light. Fact is, there's nothing at night that will hurt them any more than there is in the daylight. I think horror movies may be much of the reason for this fear.

Several years ago when my kids were young, I took a group of kids on a night hike, without lights. Actually, I had a flashlight in my pocket for any emergency, but they didn't know it. While we were planning the trip, they were really excited—kids are suckers for adventure. But as soon as we left the lights of the house, they got real quiet. Suddenly more and more little hands were touching me as we walked. Soon little voices were asking, "How much further do we have to go before we turn back? What was that? Are werewolves real? Can we *please* go back?" I stopped and said, "You don't have to be afraid. There's nothing here tonight that will hurt you—same as in the daylight." The calmness of my voice seemed to soothe them. After a few more minutes their eyes began to adjust. Lightning bugs were all around, so I said, "Let's see who can catch a lightning bug." Soon they were romping all around, laughing, playing, and catching lightning bugs in the dark. My grown kids tell me now that it was one of the most memorable nights of their childhood.

I noticed something a few nights ago that I never noticed before—the sequencing of fireflies. As I studied them, I realized that they flash three or four times in sequence, pause for a few seconds, then repeat. I live in West Tennessee. A few days later, while visiting my friend Billy Minser, who lives in East Tennessee, I discovered that fireflies there flash only once, wait about six seconds, then repeat.

After reviewing the literature, I discovered what I had suspected—different species sequence at different intervals. The most common firefly in North America, *Photinus pyralis,* flashes once, waits six seconds, then flashes again. The main purpose of the luminescence is to bring the sexes together for mating. In between flashes of the male, the female responds. This may go on until the two are close enough for physical contact, then they begin mating.

The light organ of the firefly consists of an area of transparent cuticle, under which the light-producing chemical luciferin is stored. Behind the luciferin is a layer of dense tissue that probably acts as a reflector. The enzyme involved in light production is called luciferase, and it speeds the reaction of luciferin with oxygen to produce oxyluciferin. Light is emitted as a byproduct of this reaction. Later the oxyluciferin is changed back to luciferin and the process is repeated. Oxygen is supplied to tissues in all parts of the body by a system of fine breathing tubes.

Unlike artificial lights, firefly light is produced almost entirely without heat. This makes it one of the most efficient lighting systems known—it has almost 90 percent efficiency. The average electric light bulb is only about 3 percent efficient, with 97 percent of the energy released as wasted heat. Experiments have been tried to harness chemiluminescence, but the cost has so far been prohibitive.

Fireflies don't give off much candle power. We find them so brilliant because the wave length of the light they emit happens to be the most sensitive to the human eye. In some parts of the world, people place the bugs in perforated globe lanterns to illuminate dwellings. Isn't nature wonderful?

Summer

The earth is fully awake now. The natural world is busy taking care of its young and showing off its lush growth. It's a time for shade, crystal-clear streams, and droning insects. It's a time for dew-drenched mornings, cool refreshing evenings, and night skies filled with a million stars. Humans seek air-conditioned buildings where they continue their hectic pace. Instead, nature leisurely moves to shady northern slopes with cool air currents or to the shade of submerged logs and undercut banks.

Flyfishing for Bluegills

S-smop! The water rolled and my tiny fly disappeared. I instinctively snapped my flyline taut and felt the unmistakable tug of a fat bluegill. My rod bowed and my line zinged through the dark water as if I were fighting a monster fish. I finally boated my prize, a nice dark male weighing about half a pound. Now, for you folks who occasionally net five- to ten-pound bass, that may seem small. But the fight is just about as much fun, and while on a good day you might catch five or six, I'll catch sixty to eighty. Same number of pounds, but ten to fifteen times as much fun!

Before I started flyfishing over thirty years ago, I thought bluegill fishing was for kids. Not anymore. Using the flyrod, I constantly hunt them while sculling my twelve-foot johnboat quietly around the edge of a pond

The earth is fully awake now. The natural world is busy taking care of its young and loitering in lush growth. It's a time for shade, crystal-clear streams, and droning insects. A young cotton-tailed rabbit grazes in between nursings from its mother.

or lake. I look for submerged stumps and logs, roots of overhanging trees, bank overhangs, and any other place where the water is shaded enough to be cool.

The flyrod is a unique instrument. Long and limber, it casts the weighted line, and the line itself casts the fly. In other types of casting the weight of the lure carries it out and the line follows. In flyfishing the fly is very light, and once the line is cast the fly (connected to a very light monofilament leader) follows and settles softly on the water. This is a perfect duplication of a real insect or spider settling down on the water surface. Bluegills can't resist it!

The flyreel has a different purpose than other reels, too. Its only purpose is to hold the line. That's all. I have a good quality graphite rod. It cost about forty dollars at a discount store. Of course, cheaper rods are available, as well as more expensive ones. My reel, though, is a simple manual wind-up model. It's really just a spool with a handle, and I only paid five dollars for it.

I have lots of kinds of flies (floating and sinking) and popping bugs, but my favorite—the one I use day after day—is a floating white sponge spider with rubber legs. The delicate movement of the legs seems to be especially enticing to bluegills.

Sometimes, if I'm fishing a farm pond with plenty of bass, I'll double my chances. I'll tie a medium to large popping bug about eight inches ahead of a black sinking nymph. Occasionally a bass will hit the popper while I'm waiting for the nymph to sink into a hungry bluegill's mouth. First come, first served!

Most people get the terms "bream" and "bluegill" confused. Bluegill is a distinct species of fish, *Lepomis macrochirus*. It's the one with the dark, elongated gill flap. Bream is really a name that dates back to the twelfth or thirteenth century and is said to be derived from a Teutonic word meaning "to glitter." The common bream is a freshwater fish of the carp family living in Britain and in continental Europe, as well as in Asia from Turkistan to Siberia. Bream grow to about two feet long and can weigh as much as seventeen pounds. The name bream has also been given to another member of the carp family, the white or silver bream. In this country, a more common (if incorrect) use of the term bream is any member of the panfish group, including bluegill, redear, spotted and green sunfish, warmouth, pumpkinseed, and a few others.

Fishing success depends on several factors: time of year and day, weather and water conditions, pond balance and fertility, to name a few. Fish respond most directly to their immediate environment—the water around them. Fish become more active in the spring as the water warms—bluegills begin to spawn when the water reaches 78 to 82 degrees Fahrenheit. They can be found in the shallows earlier, however. They continue to reproduce throughout the summer, and even into the fall months. In the summer, when they aren't spawning, bluegills move back to deep water where temperatures are a little cooler. Most ponds and lakes eventually stratify in the summer though, and fish can't live deeper than four to six feet because there's not enough dissolved oxygen at lower depths.

I've caught bream with the flyrod from March through October, but the best time is when they're at the height of spawning—from late May throughout the summer. You need to fish these beds quietly with little disturbance, any time of the day, but especially early morning and late evening. If you get hung or otherwise disturb the bed, wait half an hour or so and come back. Above all, don't tell anybody but your closest friends where the beds are!

On the River

I thought we never would get the boats in the water! This particular Saturday morning started early enough, with me getting up at 4:30 A.M. But after loading up, eating breakfast, and driving seventy miles to pick up my friend Mike, the sun was high. After we loaded Mike's gear and drove another forty miles to pick up Steve, it was higher still. We then drove to the launching point to unload Steve's canoe, on to the take-out point to leave

Steve's truck, then back to the launching point to unload my johnboat. When we pushed off from the bank, I looked at my watch—2:30 P.M.!

It was a lot of trouble, but we were finally on the Duck River for an afternoon of floating and fishing for smallmouth bass. And a great afternoon it was. We had scarcely gone two hundred yards when Steve tied into a two-pound "small jaws," right at the head of a series of shoals. That afternoon we caught several smallmouths, a few drums, and a few catfish. When we finally got to bed that night at Mike's house, it was nearly midnight. We got up at 5:30 A.M. and were off again, this time to the beautiful, scenic Buffalo. This trip was going to be a little different, though. This would be a two-day trip with a night spent on the river—a trip I had been looking forward to for several months.

The river is another world. Except for an occasional bridge (we crossed two in three days), it's like a wilderness area. The only people you interact with are your companions and maybe an occasional canoer. The river leaves evidence of its history, if you care to read it—and if you know the language. The bottom is covered with stones of all sizes that were once sharp, but now rounded from miles and miles of tumbling. When the floodplain flattens out, the river often forks around an island and then rejoins as the floodplain narrows. Where the river forks rejoin, the water eddies, pulling aquatic insects, crayfish, and other food items into one small area of "slack" water. This is a good place to find fish, as well as ducks. Little oxbows of still water are evidence of storm debris and rocks that clog up the entrance to a fork or a bend in the river. As time goes on, the other end is sealed off because no water is rushing through. As flowing water meets the now still water, it slows down enough to drop its rock and sediment load into the mouth of the oxbow. Fish become trapped after floods, and fishing in such areas can be quite good. Only thing is, you won't find smallmouths there because the water gets too warm. Largemouths and panfish are a good bet though. Another good place for fish and ducks is where a stream enters the river. Here again, where two bodies of flowing water meet, an eddy is formed. Other eddies can be found below boulders and log jams in the river.

Rivers teem with wildlife. Riparian (a fancy word for "streamside") vegetation usually provides abundant food, because it has plenty of moisture. Squirrels, deer, and birds are commonly seen along riverbanks. Muskrats, beavers, snakes, turtles, ducks, and other aquatic critters are abundant, too. And if you quietly ease down the river, you can often get very close to them.

Steve had to go home after the first day's float on the Buffalo; he had business to tend to the next day. But Mike and I spent the night on the river. You know, it's amazing how little you need to get by—and be quite comfortable. That night we built a fire from driftwood on a sandbar island in the middle of the river. We opened a can of stew with a hunting knife and cooked it in the can over the fire. We unfurled our bedrolls, stretched out next to the fire, and gazed at the stars. I was listing in my mind all the things I had to be thankful for as I drifted off to sleep to the soft murmuring of the nearby river.

I've taken many float trips in my time; short floats to take ducks, fish or squirrels, and long floats of over fifty miles and five days, just to relax and commune with the great outdoors. And every time I do, I wonder, why it has been so long since the last time.

Periodical Cicadas

They're kind of quiet now, but it's the first time in weeks. The evening's unusually cool for this time of year, after a storm moved through. As I write this, I'm listening from the window of my pickup in the middle of my meadow. I like to watch and listen for critters in the fading light of dusk—my favorite time of day. It's so peaceful. I'm looking at a couple of pregnant does now, their tails flicking, moving from one treeline to another across the corner of my field. All I can hear is a whippoorwill, a bullfrog and an oversexed cardinal. Yesterday, the big bugs were all I could hear; their constant droning drowned out all nature's other sounds.

They're called periodical cicadas, *Magicicada septendecim*, the big pop-eyed insects that occasionally appear in every woodlot by the thousands. These critters are multicolored, have clear wings, and are about two inches long. You may not have them where you live, but they're common throughout most of the Southeast. If you do have them in your area, I guarantee you'll know it—everybody will be talking about them. (Many folks call them "locusts.") The reason they're named "periodical" is that they emerge only once every thirteen or seventeen years, depending on the subspecies. The seventeen-year variety emerged in Tennessee in 1985. In 1989, the year I am recalling here, it was the thirteen-year subspecies. Another cicada species, the dog-day cicada, *Tibicen linnei*, emerges every year in late summer, just before opening day of squirrel season. In fact, when I first hear this cicada every year, I start hankering to get my .22 and head to the woods for bushytails.

According to a friend of mine, Dr. Randy Cate, an entomology professor at the University of Tennessee at Martin, the periodical cicadas emerge at night, after spending either thirteen or seventeen years underground. They climb up tree trunks, and after four to five days above ground, the males begin to sing to attract the females. The sound comes from vibrations of a membrane on the abdomen. After mating, females slit the bark on terminal twigs of trees and deposit their eggs. The adult insects suck sap from twigs, causing only slight damage. Eggs hatch in six to seven weeks, and the nymphs drop to the ground, burrow under, and spend the next thirteen to seventeen years sucking sap from tree roots—a long life for an insect. During their time underground, the cicadas don't do much damage to the tree. The only real damage occurs when adult females slit the terminal twigs to oviposit. This often kills the terminal buds, but usually doesn't severely damage the tree, if it's a healthy tree to begin with. I have over thirty trees in my lawn, some over two hundred years old. They're still standing and are healthy despite the cicadas. The adults only live from thirty to forty days, and most are usually gone by early July (this varies by location). These insects feed on a large variety of tree species—they especially like apple and oak trees. Entomologists estimate populations as high as thirty to forty thousand under a single large tree.

One year, my son-in-law and I went fishing at a nearby lake. We were flyfishing, using a white sponge spider with rubber legs. We noticed several cicadas buzzing around on top of the water, creating quite a commotion. We caught around twenty large bluegill and a few small bass. We thought we were doing pretty well, until we talked to another fisherman. He was bass fishing, using topwater "buzz-bait lures." He told us the bass were taking his lures like crazy, and he proved it by opening his livewell and showing us a dozen chunky bass. The largest one weighed about two pounds, but they—like ours—were all thick and heavy for their size. He said he normally released his catch, but the water was warm and they were barely alive. He offered his catch to us, and we eagerly accepted. When we cleaned all those fish (in a thunderstorm), their stomachs were full, and we were able to identify only one food item . . . "And now," as Paul Harvey would say, "you know the rest-of-the-story."

About Ticks

Uh-oh, a tick! Little rascal—stuck like a leech, sucking my blood. If you spend time outdoors during warm months, you're going to occasionally feed a tick or two. How serious is it? I've heard you can get a new disease. How do I get ticks? What can I do to protect myself? You've probably asked these questions at one time or another. Here are some answers.

Of the sixteen kinds of ticks in the southeastern United States, the lone star tick, *Amblyomma americanum,* and the American dog tick, *Dermacentor variabilis,* are the most troublesome. The female lone star tick has a single white spot in the middle of its back and has been identified as a carrier of Rocky Mountain spotted fever west of the Mississippi River. In Tennessee, this disease is transmitted by the American dog tick. It is mahogany-colored with white mottling. The lone star tick is especially troublesome following the egg hatch in July, when the tiny larvae, called "seed ticks," attach by the hundreds to any passerby. They burrow into the skin and cause itching and swelling that can last for weeks. The American dog tick is not as prevalent as the lone star tick.

The immature stages do not attack people, but the adult will readily attach to a human host and may transmit Rocky Mountain spotted fever.

Ticks are extremely well equipped to suck blood. Experts say that the mouth includes borers, hooks, lancets, and tubes, along with other miscellaneous items. (I don't know what these items are—the other tools sound bad enough.) The tick bores its whole head into you—this is why they are so hard to dislodge. Ticks don't have many natural enemies and are not greatly affected by weather. Their respiratory system is located on the body just behind the rear legs. They are resistant to insecticides, because they are not insects—they belong to the same family as scorpions and mites. All ticks require blood to mature and complete the reproductive cycle. But they are extremely patient in getting blood. Young ticks can live a year without feeding, and adults can live three years. After a female tick reproduces, she dies, but there is good news as well as bad news. The bad news is that she can lay up to four thousand eggs before she dies; the good news is that fewer than 5 percent of the young will live to maturity.

Even though the worst thing that can happen from most tick bites is itching around the bite, it is well known that ticks can carry a number of typhus-like diseases. Rocky Mountain spotted fever is the best known of these, but in recent years, Lyme disease has caused problems as well. This disease is caused by a spirochete found in the blood of many mammals and birds, particularly deer. It causes several symptoms, including flulike symptoms, a rash, nausea, a stiff neck, fever, or pain and swelling of the joints. Some people may experience more severe symptoms, such as nerve disorders, inflammation of the heart, and heart block. Lyme disease is very serious, but early detection and treatment with antibiotics usually cures it and prevents its return.

So, how do you protect yourself? No need to stop going outdoors during tick season. Just be aware and follow these tips:

(1) In tick-infested areas, wear protective clothing and spray your boots, socks and pants with a repellent spray which has Permethrin or Deet (N, N-diethyl-m-toluamide) as the main ingredient.

(2) If you don't have a repellent, tuck your pants legs into your boots and put a strip of tape—sticky side out—around each leg at about mid-thigh height and each upper arm. Ticks crawl up toward the trunk of your body, so you can catch them on the tape.

(3) If you do find a tick attached, gently pull it off (its head, too!) and disinfect the area. The sooner the tick is removed the better. It may take several hours for a tick to infect a person. According to an article by H. G. Lendle, in *Nature Society News,* putting nail polish, salad oil, or turpentine on a tick to make it turn loose is a mistake. A tick doesn't breathe through its head, and all you would do is kill it, leaving it still attached. A tick can't withdraw its head, even if it

wants to, until it is full of blood. Once the tick sinks its head into you, it secretes a cement that keeps the head firmly in place. After becoming full, it secretes a second substance to dissolve the cement.

(4) Carefully watch the area where the tick was removed. If a red circular rash appears, see a doctor immediately.

(5) Lyme disease is a relatively new disease to the South. Many doctors are not aware of the disease, and this fact may cause delay in proper treatment. Therefore, inform your doctor of the possibility; a simple blood test can confirm, but not necessarily reject the possibility of Lyme disease.

One spring, during a turkey hunt in Missouri, I found a tick embedded under my left arm. I carefully removed it and watched the bite area over the next two days while I hunted. The area remained red and irritated. Upon arriving home, I went to my doctor to have it checked. She pulled a blood sample, and after a couple of days it proved to be negative for Lyme disease or Rocky Mountain spotted fever. The doctor explained that a positive test would have been conclusive, but unfortunately a negative test was not. She put me on antibiotics for fourteen days—one pill four times per day, on an empty stomach—and no milk products at all. That meant no ice cream! I love ice cream. This experience made me realize two things: my habit of eating small meals regularly with snacks in between leaves my stomach empty very seldom, and I didn't realize just how much I would miss my cereal with milk in the morning and my favorite snack, frozen yogurt. She also suggested that I stay inside out of the sun. No way! Not for two weeks. Anyway, the antibiotic treatment was a precaution. She told me that as long as the treatment was done early (within a few days after the bite) there was no danger of getting either disease. I survived, everything's fine, and I'm eating frozen yogurt again.

For dog owners, *Arkansas Outdoors* magazine offers this tip to protect hunting dogs from ticks without dipping the dogs in smelly, messy solutions every week or so. Not only will this be easier for you, but the dog no doubt will prefer this method: simply add two tablespoons of a brewer's yeast–garlic powder mix to your dog's food every day. This mix is available at most health food stores. For finicky dogs, there is even a cheese-flavored variety. I don't know if it works or not, but it sounds like a neat idea.

Frog Hunting: A Good Way to Spend a Summer Night

There are lots of ways to spend a summer night, but there's nothing like spending it outdoors. And of all the enjoyable things to do outdoors on a summer night, frog hunting is near the top of my list.

The United States has many kinds of frogs (there are twenty-one in Tennessee alone), but in most areas, the only one legal to hunt is the bullfrog,

Rana catesbeiana. It's basically found throughout the eastern half of the country, except for the southern tip of Florida. The hind legs are about the only meaty part, but a large frog has large legs, and they are truly a delicacy.

But let's not get ahead of ourselves. Before we can eat them, we have to find them. Finding them is not too hard though, after the weather warms up. Most nights, all you have to do is to get close to a body of water and listen. Their familiar "jug-a-rum" call is hard to confuse with any other night sounds. Once you've located a few you're in business.

Your equipment can be as simple or as complex as you want to make it. Basically, though, you need a light, something to catch or kill them with, and something to put them in. I like to keep things simple. For a light, I have a headlight with a six-volt lantern battery I carry in a holder on my belt. This leaves both hands free. I use a king-size pillowcase to carry the frogs in—the larger size leaves plenty of room to tie a knot in the top. It also give the frogs plenty of room.

One year some 4-H members and I caught a few large bullfrogs we planned to have for breakfast the next morning. Several 4-H'ers and a few adult volunteer leaders were sleeping in a cabin—some of us on the floor and some on cots. Since everyone was already asleep when we got in from the hunt, we quietly got undressed and went to bed without a light. I put the wet sack of frogs on the floor at the end of my cot. Next morning my sack of frogs was all the way across the room *and* out on the edge of the twelve-foot-high deck, tied to a post. I awoke to the buzzing of two adult leaders who hadn't gone on the frog hunt with us. "What kind of snake do you think he's got in that bag?" one said. The other answered: "I don't know, but he must be a fierce rascal. I woke up to 'im striking at my arm. I knew he must've been Dr. Byford's, so I carefully dragged 'im back over to his cot. I managed to doze back off, but not an hour later he was back again, striking with a vengeance. He must be *really* mean. This time I dragged 'im over and tied him to that post with a string. But I tell you, I didn't sleep anymore the rest of the night!" When I told them the sack was filled with bullfrogs that had been able to travel across the room by "leapfrogging" each other in the roomy sack, we all had a good laugh. The kids loved it.

People catch or kill frogs in different ways. Some use a .22 rifle, but this can be dangerous, because bullets easily ricochet off water. One good method is to gig them with a four-prong barbed gig on the end of a fishing cane. Another way is to simply catch them by hand. This is a little harder, but with practice and a lot of patience it can be done. The secret is to get into the water and move along the shoreline, about four to six feet out. You need to move slowly and look carefully. When you see one large enough to eat, quietly and slowly move closer, keeping the light rigidly on the frog at all times. Try not to make many ripples in the water and never put your hands in front of the light. If two or more people are together, all but one should turn off their lights. When you're close enough for the grab, brace yourself by slowly kneeling to one knee or getting your feet squarely under you. Move both hands slowly from outside the light inward toward the frog. When you're in comfortable grabbing distance, grab suddenly with both hands, placing them squarely over the frog to pin it down. Getting close enough to gig frogs is done the same way, except you don't have to get quite as close.

The position of the frog is important. Sometimes they're on the bank, from within inches of the water to six or eight feet from it. Sometimes they're in vegetation, other times on a lily pad, log, or other object. Often part of the body will be in the water and part out. Again, they'll often be in aquatic vegetation, but not always. It's easier to catch them if they're facing the bank. If they're facing the water, and you miss or scare them, they'll escape by jumping around you into the water—then it's over. I prefer the frog to be dry. It seems they're more reluctant to jump back into the water if they're dry—like sunbathers. I also prefer them to be in vegetation. They seem to think they're hidden that way, and if they think they're hidden, you have a better chance of getting close. In fact, the easiest frogs to catch are the ones that slowly submerge in shallow water and flatten themselves out on the bottom. These always think they're hidden.

Several years ago, a good friend and I were conducting in-service training at a rural Holiday Inn. That night, he and I went frog hunting. We each caught our limit of 10 and returned to the motel. Since we were tired, we decided to wait until coffee break next morning to dress them. We put the two sacks of frogs into garbage cans with ice around them. (Frogs are quite comfortable and less active when cold.) Next morning, I was waiting my turn at the podium when I heard a scream and looked out the sliding-glass door. The maid was running out of our room. Needless to say, I quickly retrieved the frogs, and we had our coffee break early that morning!

There are several ways to cook frog legs. My favorite way is very simple. After killing the frogs and removing the legs, skin them and cut off the feet. (Some people leave the feet on.) Roll them in flour, salt lightly, and fry in melted margarine until they're golden brown. Drain on paper towels and serve hot. Delicious!

One of the neat things about frog hunting is seeing the abundance of aquatic life at night. Fish in the shallows, their fins slowly undulating, are mesmerized by the light. Water snakes slither through the reeds, enjoying the cool, damp conditions when fish and frogs—their primary prey—are more active. Mud and musk turtles scurry under the decaying vegetation. Spiders glow in their mystical woven silks. Broods of downy ducklings under the nervous, watchful eye of their mother paddle reluctantly away, curious at this strange intrusion. It's all a wonderful world that few people ever see.

Heartworms: Don't Get Caught Napping

I'm reminded of a young man who stayed out late at night and had to go to work early the next morning. He went, but about mid-morning, he couldn't hold his head up anymore, so he laid his head down—on his hands—on the desk. His boss came in to bring him some papers. As soon as the young man heard the door open, he slowly raised his head and said, "Amen."

Slick trick, and that might have worked on his boss. But if your dog gets heartworms, by the time you discover it, it may be too late. I was lucky with Penny. Penny was just a mixed-up mutt (in terms of bloodlines, that is), but somehow in that weird concoction of DNA, genes, and chromosomes, the good Lord put together one of the finest squirrel dogs I've ever seen. She hunted with her eyes, ears, and nose.

A few years ago, I took Penny in to the clinic to get her shots and generally checked over. I felt smug. I was taking care of my dog—once a year check-up, whether she needs it or not. She runs free all year so she can stay tuned up on squirrels. Back when I grew up, folks never took their dogs to vets, and they seemed to do OK. But I wasn't taking any chances, because Penny was one of those once-in-a-lifetime dogs.

Dr. Huey Claybrook looked her over, gave her shots, and said, "Jim, do you give her a heartworm preventative?" I answered, "Why—no I don't—do you think I ought to?" If he'd been wearing glasses he would've glared over the rim at me. He said, "Mind if I check her?" I quickly agreed, and he drew a blood sample from her front leg. Putting a tiny drop on a slide, he immediately placed it under a microscope. The whole process took about two minutes. "Too late," he said. These words hit me like a ton of bricks. "Come take a look." I looked through the scope at dozens of squirming, threadlike larvae, "Microfilaria," he said, "immature heart worms. The adults are much larger. They're in the heart, and they're the ones doing the damage." Dr. Joe Adcock walked in and showed me a preserved specimen of an infected dog's heart, with a portion of the wall cut away. It was packed with what looked like spaghetti, except the worms were about the diameter of pencil lead. Joe told me that the parasite is bad news, that it will usually kill the dog, sometimes as long as four years after infestation. Huey told me he couldn't guarantee a successful treatment, but he would try if I wanted him to. It was a long involved process and would be expensive. I assured him I wanted him to try.

Heartworms, found worldwide, are always harmful and sometimes fatal. The heartworm parasite, *Dirofilaria immitis,* is transmitted in the immature stage by mosquitoes. Small immature heartworms are deposited in the bloodstream after the dog is bitten by an infected mosquito. The tiny parasites travel to the dog's heart, and there in the next six to seven months, grow to adult worms that may reach a length of ten to twelve inches. Female adults then release larval worms into the bloodstream. Mosquitoes that draw blood from the infected dog are capable of transmitting the parasite to other dogs, thereby continuing the heartworm life cycle.

Because the southern states have the most mosquitoes, heartworms are more common here. However, interstate transportation of dogs has carried the parasite to all regions of the United States, including Hawaii, and into southern Canada.

Heartworms can be prevented by oral medications that kill the immature worms. One type of medication is given daily, and another is given only once per month—all year long. However, the drug must be given only to dogs free from the parasite; otherwise, a fatal shock syndrome can occur. Therefore, all dogs should be screened for heartworms before being placed on a preventative program.

Penny went through the entire treatment and then was placed on a once-a-month preventative program. The treatment went like this. First she was given an arsenic compound to kill the adult worms. She expelled the worms into her lungs and contracted pneumonia. Huey told me this always happens. About three days after the treatment, I gave her two pills twice daily for ten days to keep the pneumonia complications down. She went back to the vet for a second treatment, this time to kill the immature worms. She got to come back home for ten days, then she returned to the vet for a final check.

Huey and Joe told me I was lucky, probably because they caught the condition in time, and because Penny was a young dog. After her recovery, Penny got a pill a month and a pat on the head every day. She lived several years after that. And on those clear, crisp winter mornings, even in her older years, she always met me at the door, head cocked and tail wagging, as if asking, "Where's the rifle?"

Fall

Surely there's not a greater time to be alive than fall. Nature's crop is not only "laid by"—it's ripe for the picking. Leaves have spent their season gathering food for the seeds, with enough extra to store in the roots. Now in hues of orange and yellow, their life work complete, they drift lazily down to their final resting place. Nature's young are not quite grown, but their independence from mother makes them think they are. Mornings are crisp, and evenings are cool—and the brilliance and warmth of midday seem to put a bounce in the weakest of steps. Meanwhile, critters gorge on abundant food, laying on layers of fat to help them survive the winter ahead.

Signs of Fall

Fall has always been my favorite time since I was a youngster. One of the reasons was that my birthday falls in September; it was also when I would begin hunting with my dad. County fair season and even going back to school with new clothes and seeing my friends again were factors, too. But, there's more to it than that. It's the change, the excitement of change.

Yesterday, I went dove hunting. Birds didn't fly until 4:00 p.m., but I got there at noon. And as I sat there on the hill, enjoying the peace and beauty of East Tennessee, I became thankful I was able to see, hear, smell, and even feel the seasons changing.

Actually, I begin sensing fall earlier than most folks tell me they do. By mid-July I can smell maturing vegetation in the woods and fields. It has lost the lush, bright green look of spring and now is summer-worn and leathery. By late July, I begin to notice cicadas singing in mid-morning. This has always been a signal to me that it's time to quit the morning squirrel hunt, because squirrels become inactive when the temperature warms up enough for cicadas to sing. These signs are subtle at first, but they're there, and if you're outdoors enough and take the time, you can sense them.

The young of wildlife species begin to "bunch up" near the nesting area as they grow away from their parents. Starlings and doves are good examples. You can begin to see large concentrations by mid-July—and if food is plentiful, they will stick around until they're ready to head south, when the weather gets colder and days get shorter. These early concentrations of doves are the ones we hunt in the opening weeks of dove season. I get several calls from irate homeowners at this time of year, because young starlings like to roost in dense shade trees around folks' homes. And, of course, they leave their sign—on cars, sidewalks, lawns, and sometimes people. Lots of people want to get rid of the birds when this happens, which is understandable, but it's usually not worth the effort, because the birds will leave on their own in a few weeks.

As the early fall progresses, nights become cool and the afternoons warm. This is a special kind of warm, because the humidity is low. During these conditions, snakes move more. Several years ago when I was a wildlife specialist with the Agricultural Extension Service, I could predict by my calendar when I would begin to get snake calls in the office. Snakes appear in folks' homes, around their homes, and move across their lawns, simply because the snakes feel like moving. They are feeding heavily on abundant populations of rodents, insects, and other animal life that have built up during summer. All this food becomes fat reserves in preparation for hibernation.

Some species have their young in the fall as well. A few years ago about September 7, a squirrel hunter called to tell me he'd found five rattlesnakes and three copperheads together on a large rock outcropping under a boulder. He shot the snakes, and young snakes began to crawl out of the mothers' bodies. He kept shooting until he killed all of them. (Too bad he did that, but the ethics of killing snakes is fodder for another story.) Each mother had from six to eight young inside her, and the pregnant females had gathered near the den site in September to have their young. The young and parents would have denned together in the winter, then emerged and gone separate ways the next spring. Rattlesnakes and copperheads often den together during the winter. You are more likely to see these species during the fall than at any other time, as they move toward their dens. Some other snakes have their young this time of year, too.

Even in poor years, fall provides a bounty of food for man and other animals. Nuts, acorns, fruit, crops, and game are all at their peak. Nature prepares this bounty every year for harvest, and what's not harvested will return to the soil to enrich it for the next year's crop. Plant eaters, such as rabbits, deer, and squirrels, are eager to shift from summer greens to these new foods, as they become available. Deer, for example, subsist on green twigs and leaves, which are tender and succulent during the spring and early summer. But by late summer, when the vegetation becomes hard and leathery, they're quite ready to change to new foods, such as acorns, persimmons, wild grapes, and crops. Movement patterns change suddenly and often this time of year.

About the end of September, I always make my annual trek to the woods to bowhunt for deer. A week later, I'll sit in my treestand and watch the early October multicolored leaves dance to the ground. Shivering slightly in the cool morning air and basking in the afternoon sunshine, I'll once again be thankful. I'll reflect on what I've known—really since I was a child. The land will feed us forever, as long as we treat it with loving care and respect. Ah, the fall—what a glorious time to be alive!

What Squirrels Eat

What a fine weekend of hunting grey squirrels! Saturday, opening morning, found me easing along a dry creekbed in Humphreys County, Tennessee, watching and listening for bushytails. I normally hunt the northern slopes where the hickories grow tall and straight, but a brief scouting trip Friday afternoon revealed few nuts and little squirrel sign. My mind was drifting back to opening mornings as a boy. Times I loved—the misty cool of a late summer morning and the smell of squirrels and gunpowder. I knew Uncle Ernest's woods like the back of my hand—better. The shake of a dogwood tree about thirty yards ahead brought me back to the present. The young grey swished the tiny limb looking for another cluster of red, when my crosshairs settled on his head. My first squirrel of the season.

Saturday morning, I found squirrels feeding on dogwood, blackgum, and ironwood (hophornbeam). While they are more active feeding on these small seeds than when cutting hickory nuts, they are also much quieter. And unless you're careful, they can see you before you see them, because they're not far from the ground.

I first noticed squirrels feeding on ironwood over twenty years ago. I had spent most of the morning hunting ridges with little luck. Hickories had produced poorly that year and squirrels were scarce. I dropped off one ridge to a little stream bottom I remembered having some good hickory trees a few years before. Maybe there were more nuts in the bottoms than on the ridges. As I got closer to the bottom, my heart sank. The little bottom had been clearcut! The only trees standing were half a dozen three- to four-inch ironwood saplings. I was impressed though, by the lush stand of jewelweed; it was beautiful. As I walked a little closer, I heard a steady drone. Closer inspection revealed perhaps a hundred hummingbirds buzzing the showy spotted orange jewelweed blossoms! I was enthralled—I'd never seen this many hummingbirds in one place. I stood there in wonder for maybe ten minutes, when suddenly the tops of the little ironwood trees came alive with grey squirrels. I couldn't believe my eyes: there were two to three in each of those tiny three- to four-inch trees. I finished my limit of ten squirrels by taking seven from those few trees.

Saturday afternoon, I drove to the other side of the county, about twenty miles away. Here I found a different situation. Hickories on the ridges *were* producing nuts, and squirrels were in them. I finished my limit of ten easily. I also found a few squirrels cutting red oak acorns and beech mast.

Mast (hard-seeded fruit and nuts) production is fickle. Weather seems to have more effect than anything else on production from year to year. Summer drought and early spring freezes take their toll. Microclimates can vary from one side of the county to another, from one ridge to another, and even from the bottom to the top of the same ridge.

I've seen squirrels feed on a variety of other foods during the hunting season: tupelo gum and cypress balls in the bottoms, sweetgum balls, poplar cones, pine cones, maple seed, muscadines, walnuts, corn, acorns from several kinds of oaks, and pecans. In early spring, squirrels eat buds, bark, flowers, and almost any other source of food during this critical period. They also smell out leftover nuts and acorns they buried in the fall for winter food.

A mature grey squirrel eats from one to two pounds of food a week, which adds up to about one hundred pounds per year. During years of critical mast shortage, and when there are large numbers of squirrels, they develop "shock disease," a condition caused by low levels of sugar in the blood. Squirrels in this condition will travel for miles looking for food, swimming rivers and crossing highways by the thousands. In Tennessee, 1968 was the most recent year for a large "squirrel migration." Since then, there have been years with poor food and other years with high squirrel numbers, but not at the same time.

Good Fall Mast Means More Fawns

I've seen good mast years and poor mast years. I've seen some years when you couldn't find an acorn at all—and others when you could hardly walk in the woods without crunching acorns.

Mast is actually a term for any hard-seeded fruit or nut produced by trees or shrubs. The most common type of mast, though, is acorns. It's been recognized for many years that acorns and other mast are extremely critical to wildlife. In fact, a deer will eat up to two and one-half pounds of acorns a day. And sixty to eighty pounds of acorns per acre are needed to support a healthy population of deer, squirrels, quail, and turkeys. All of us know that an animal survives only if it has food to eat all year long. The interesting thing about most mast crops such as acorns is that even when they're abundant they're often gone by late winter. During the late winter, deer don't usually have much to eat at all. They'll nibble on honeysuckle now and then and a few other plants that stay green throughout the year, but there's not much to eat during late winter. How is it, then, that a good mast year can have much effect on a fawn crop?

If you ask that question to a sheep farmer, he could probably tell you after he thought about it a little. I've raised sheep, and I've noticed that some parallels between sheep and deer are surprisingly close. Sheep are seasonal breeders, like deer. They don't breed at all until the day length becomes just right. This is called photoperiodism. When the day length shortens to the proper time, a nerve center in the brain signals the testes in the ram and the ovaries in the ewe to produce certain hormones that stimulate the reproductive urge. Now, sheep farmers know when this is and so do wildlife biologists. Sheep farmers plan for it. They turn the ram in with the ewes to maximize or hit the photoperiod just right. About three weeks before they turn the ram in, they begin to feed the ewes more food at a higher plane of nutrition. This is called flushing the ewes. What it means is this. If a ewe is gaining weight when she ovulates, she will produce more eggs. When the ram fertilizes the ewe with thousands of sperm, there's a better chance that more lambs will be conceived. After breeding, for most of the gestation period, the ewe doesn't need a high plane of nutrition. Even though there are developing lambs inside her, they are tiny, and she can do just fine on a high-roughage diet with low protein. She can do well on such a diet until just before she gets ready to drop her lambs. Now, during the last three or four weeks of pregnancy, there's a tremendous strain on the ewe's body—to put the final touches on developing those now large lambs. So the sheep farmer has to begin feeding the ewes a high-protein, low-roughage ration again. To maximize income, then, the shepherd feeds a high-protein ration just before breeding and just before lambing, and he feeds a low-protein, high-roughage ration in between.

Now the parallel with deer. Though research has yet to prove it, common sense tells me that deer reproduction is exactly the same. A high-protein, high-energy ration is needed just before the bucks breed the does, and just before the fawns are dropped. This gives us a good fawn crop. And all during the intervening six months, deer can survive on a very low protein, low-energy ration. Now, the good Lord had it figured out pretty well. During most mast years, there's plenty of high-protein, high-energy food available just before does are bred—usually around November. (In the Deep South, they're actually bred a little later.) Acorns play out, though, as the winter progresses, and the gestation period progresses. And then, just before fawning (May in most areas, later in the Deep South), there's plenty of summer's green browse to fill up on, to put the does on a high nutritional plane. The intervening months, again, are not so important. During winter, when there's not much food, deer reproduction doesn't seem to suffer.

One of the reasons deer do so well in agricultural areas is that there is plenty of grain, soybeans, or other food crops available during the fall—every year. These agricultural foods provide the nutrition to flush the does, and reproduction seems to be good every year. But in heavily forested situations, the fawn crop is dependent on the quality of the mast year. So when you see a good mast year, it means our deer herd is going to be on the upswing.

Find the Hottest Food, and You've Found the Deer

The day was mostly cloudy as we headed into the big woods of Humphreys County. It was only 9:00 A.M., but it was already hot and muggy—sure didn't seem right that deer archery season was just a week away! Some people scout for deer during the summer, and that's fine if you want to find a deer population, or nail down the home range of a big buck. But don't put your stand up until just before you're ready to hunt. Why? Well, it's a long story. The bottom line though, is that in early fall, deer may be here today and gone tomorrow. Or, stated in scientific terms, they shift their core areas often.

All summer they usually have plenty to eat. Green vegetation abounds everywhere—succulent forbs, green twigs and leaves of hardwood trees and shrubs, tender leafy vines, and grass. Deer love these foods, but after they've eaten them all spring and summer, they're ready for something different—very ready. After all, I love ice cream, but enough is enough. Now, it so happens that in the fall, about when most state bow seasons begin, new highly preferred foods become available: acorns, muscadines, persimmons, corn, crabapples, just to name a few. And as soon as the first few fall—whoosh! They draw deer like jelly draws flies. This is when deer leave most of their summer trails and wander throughout their home range until they find these new foods. Then, they settle in for a while—a few days or maybe a week or two. During this time they may continuously occupy an area no larger than ten to fifteen acres (sometimes more) of their 250-plus-acre home range. This smaller area is called a core area. When conditions become better in another part of their range, they will shift their activity to that part and establish another core area. Food is most often the thing that determines a deer's core area, but other factors are sometimes involved, such as rutting behavior or nursing a newborn fawn. If you locate a hot feeding spot, chances are you've located the core area of several deer, all with overlapping home ranges.

I was able to document this phenomenon in Alabama nearly thirty years ago, while gathering data for my doctoral research. Radio telemetry was a new tool back then, and I was using it to monitor the effects of logging on deer movement. On this particular occasion, it was late winter (February 9, 1968) when I caught No. 3071 (a doe) at the edge of a food plot. She, along with several other deer, had been forced out of the bottomland for a couple of months by high water. This upland grass/clover plot was one of the last food sources available, and it was nearly gone. For almost a week, every time I would pick up her signal, she would be either in or near the food plot. One morning I returned to the area and found she had moved to a location about a half mile away. Every two hours I turned on the receiver and found her still in the new location. Time to check this out. I dreaded what I might find, possibly that she had been killed and the radio transmitter collar was lying on the ground sending signals. As I approached the radio signal, she jumped up and bounded away—then I discovered why she wasn't moving. The local hunting club had strewn several truckloads of ear corn down about a half mile of old logging road. No need to move; she had all she needed right there. For the next two weeks, she had a very small core area around that corn. But the corn didn't last long. Deer, turkeys, squirrels, raccoons, and birds soon cleaned it up—groceries were scarce. No. 3071 began to move in a wandering manner within a third portion of her range, away from the food plot and the old ear corn site. Close inspection revealed that the water in the bottom was receding and spring greenery in that south Alabama woods was beginning to unfold. After about a week of this wandering, she established a third core area in the bottom, where new green lushness was abundant. She stayed in that core area for about a month, and that's when my radio died.

I've used this core area concept while hunting for years now. I look for the newest most preferred food available—at the time I want to hunt. Finding last week's sign is no good, unless yesterday's sign is there as well. I look for *fresh* droppings. If I can also find droppings from other days as well; that's even better. When I take a deer I check the rumen for key foods. This often helps me zero in on feeding areas.

My scouting on the muggy day I mentioned earlier paid off. Even though choice foods (mostly acorns) were abundant, I found a couple of chestnut oak trees that had been dropping acorns earlier than most, and deer sign that ranged from two weeks old to the day before. When I tagged the nice spike, I checked the stomach. Mostly acorns, chestnut oak, post oak, white oak—OK, that doesn't surprise me; miscellaneous leaves—no surprises—they always have some browse. But wait—what's this? Crabapple, and another, and another! But they're not falling yet—at least not where I've been. Hmmm. They obviously are somewhere though. Time to scout a little more and find that crabapple tree—for next weekend.

Common Sense Scouting

Scouting for game is part of the hunt as far as I'm concerned. I've been invited on hunts where the host already had a place picked out for me, but a hunt never seems complete unless I scout for the game myself.

I know some hunters who stay in the woods all year, but my scouting time is limited. So I generally do most of my scouting just before or during the hunt. Besides, as I've pointed out before, game movements vary during the year. The animals constantly shift their activity to areas within their home range where food, water, and cover are most abundant at the time. The frequency of these shifts varies from season to season. For example, in early fall when acorns, persimmons, and other mast begin to drop, deer may change their location weekly, sometimes even daily.

A few years ago, a week before bow season, I found a "hot spot" under a grove of persimmon trees. Four different deer trails—and fresh tracks and droppings were everywhere! My adrenaline was flowing as I set up an old ladder stand I had stored in the barn. The setup was perfect. It was within walking distance of my house, and I could get in a couple hours of hunting every morning before work. I could hardly sleep the night before opening morning. That morning I slipped quietly into my stand and hoisted my bow. As the sun's first rays began to make the ground visible, I was confident I would be hauling my deer out within an hour. But as the hours passed, I knew something was wrong. About 10:30 I climbed down to check the sign. Was I surprised to find *no* fresh tracks or droppings! My neighbor had a cornfield about a quarter mile away and on a hunch I headed toward the field. Sure enough, he had harvested his corn during the past week. I took a shortcut through the woodlot to a field corner I had found deer using a couple of years before. As I eased up to the field, I spotted three bucks and four does. A freshly harvested cornfield will draw deer about as quickly as any feature food I know.

The biggest advantage of scouting all year is becoming familiar with the terrain. But if your scouting time is limited, how can you maximize your efforts? If I'm hunting an area I'm not familiar with, I'll first look the area over in what I term "macro-scouting" fashion. I'll drive through the area I plan to hunt and look for unique land features and habitat types. When I find a spot that looks interesting, I'll hurriedly check it out. If I find sign, I'll mark the spot on my topo map, get into my truck, and look for another. After I've found several likely spots or covered the whole area, I'll go back to each spot where I found sign and scout them in more detail ("micro-scouting").

I actually prefer to hunt far from any road, but often I don't have the time to scout such areas. If I do, I'll don a backpack and spend two or three days scouting such remote areas. These areas are less hunted by other folks and provide the most satisfying hunts for me. But again, with limited time I don't often have this luxury. Macro-scouting may not be the best way, but it works. And if you want to make the best of your time, it may be the best alternative. Good luck!

Filming a Bowhunting Video

As a wildlife biologist and outdoorsman, I've had my share of exciting adventure. I've canoed, johnboated, and rafted whitewater and back water of several states, hiked remote mountain trails in the Smokies, the Rockies, and the Sierras. I've bowhunted, gun-hunted, and muzzleloader-hunted several species of North American game and once stood face-to-face with a Colorado bear at ten yards—with bow in hand. I've seen wildlife do some amazing things and had many outdoor thrills. Sometimes I've been able to share experiences with a companion, but most often the only record I have are my memories, because I was alone. But a few years ago, I had an experience that will be shared by thousands of people—at least most of the experience will be shared.

It all started one summer. While in my office shuffling paper, I received a call from a video company in Alaska called Alaskan Wilderness Perspectives. Wade Nolan, its president, wanted to film a video on bowhunting white-tailed deer in the eastern United States. The featured habitat was to be the "patchwork quilt," referring to broken terrain (patches) of agricultural crops, standing timber, clearcut timber, and abandoned fields and homesteads. I eagerly accepted, because I'm a sucker for a new adventure.

We set a date in late October to meet at the Deer Creek Hunting Lodge near Sebree, Kentucky. At the time, this lodge was owned and operated by Tim Stull and Robert Gillham. They leased about twenty-five hundred acres of prime whitetail habitat from area farmers and catered to only bowhunters, farm game hunters, and waterfowl hunters. They provided comfortable lodging, excellent food, and, for an extra fee, a guide service. Because bowhunting was the only way they allowed whitetails to be taken, several bucks were allowed to reach the age to have large racks. Consequently, they boast a sizable number of Pope and Young record-book animals taken in the last few years. Wade and a few of his crew met me at the lodge late one evening, and we planned our filming strategy. Wade and two of his film crew left for Missouri the next day, leaving Keith, one of the cameramen, to work with me for the next couple of days.

The next day we spent several hours filming all aspects of deer habitat. I commented on deer behavior, biology, movement ecology, and hunting techniques. One aspect of the taping involved me scouting for a bowhunting stand site, explaining where to scout, how to scout, and then actually choosing a site for my treestand. Once I selected a site, I erected my treestand and Keith located his in another tree about eight yards away, slightly higher than my stand. It was a beautiful spot in a wide swath of bedding cover, near a beaver swamp between a soybean field and a cornfield. Deer had prominent intersecting trails, one parallel to each field edge and one between the two fields. We predetermined which directions Keith could film my shooting a deer, and finally, about dark, we were all set.

The next morning was beautiful for hunting, even though the temperature wasn't very cold. After we both settled into our stands, Keith used quite a bit of film, taping a beautiful sunrise, squirrels, woodpeckers, and migrating warblers. Keith is a great cameraman to film a bowhunting adventure, because he's a bowhunter himself, and thus understands the importance of camouflage and minimizing movement, sound, and human smell. It was about 7:45 A.M. when I noticed movement to my right. A spike buck came into view, and since Keith was positioned to my left he didn't see the deer. By the time I got Keith's attention, the spike was only twenty yards away and there was a seven-point buck with him! The spike had heard my low whistle to Keith and was a little nervous, but began to cross the narrow slough anyway. The seven-point followed and instantly they were only ten yards behind my stand, where I couldn't shoot. Keith turned the camera on and the nervous spike heard it and ran back across the slough. The seven-point heard the camera but had not heard my whistle, so he looked at the retreating spike in puzzlement. He looked all around for the camera noise, but not able to see anything suspicious he settled down and milled around behind my stand. Eventually he turned and headed right for my tree, passing within two yards of it, directly under me! Keith continued filming, but I couldn't shoot because of a limb. As the buck moved out in front of my stand into the open, I waited until he lowered his head, then drew my bow. He was quartering away at fifteen yards when I shot. The hit was perfect, passing through both lungs. He bounded out about forty yards and collapsed, still within view. He was dead in about forty-five seconds. I was elated. I looked at Keith and he was limp, confused, and deflated. He had run out of film about two seconds before the arrow hit the deer! Keith was obviously distraught. He had used too much of the cartridge filming the sights and sounds of the swamp that morning. As it turned out, he was using a camera unfamiliar to him. He had expected a warning light a few minutes before the tape ran out, but this particular one didn't have that feature.

After reloading, he filmed me as I reconstructed the shot. He filmed me climbing out of the tree and trailing the animal. I couldn't be upset, because of feeling sorry for Keith. He was a victim of Murphy's law.

The buck was a fat, healthy specimen. One antler had a broken point, but he field-dressed at 135 pounds. It was a beautiful morning, and the whole experience was a thrill for me.

Winter

It's cold now, and times are tough for the natural world. Some spend the frigid days asleep with reduced metabolism. Some tough it out, seeking scarce food almost constantly, and retreating to burrows or windbreaks for needed rest. The strong with sufficient fat reserves make it; the weak do not. Some, the ones that stored fall food with industry, eat well during winter. They're not really smarter, they just have a better survival instinct. Most don't have that evolutionary advantage.

Deer Sometimes Pattern Hunters—Dare to Be Different

It was getting colder by the minute. The morning had been dreary, wet, and, in general, miserable. There had been snow a couple of days before. This morning had seen rain at about 35 degrees, but now the temperature was plummeting, causing the rain to turn to sleet. By 2:00 p.m. there was a sheet of ice over a packed snow base. I was soaking wet, freezing, and facing the prospect of getting stranded on the last day of a December bow season—in the middle of Tennessee's Land-Between-the-Lakes. The weather forecast predicted below-zero temperature that night with no thaw in sight. I hated to forego the last afternoon of the season, but knew I had to get out of there while I still could—if I could. As I was slipping and sliding up a hill in my two-wheel-drive, my mind was going over my options. If I could reach the main four-lane highway which bordered the hunting area, the traffic might be keeping the road clear. I could then hunt during the afternoon without risk of being stranded for gosh-knows how long. Sure enough, I finally made it out and found clear tire tracks. If I was careful I could make it. The sleet had stopped, but the temperature was now already below zero and still going down. I pulled over, quickly changed to dry clothes, and proceeded slowly down the four-lane road. I was looking for thick honeysuckle cover. I knew deer would be there for two reasons. This late in the season, deer have been heavily pressured by both gun hunters and bowhunters, and they would be in the thickets for refuge. Also, by this time, honeysuckle was one of the few foods left. Finally, deer would probably move some because all the other hunters had already gone home. Soon I found the spot I was looking for—a thick honeysuckle tangle in a hollow leading away from the road. I pulled over, took two steps off the shoulder, and there it was—a fresh set of big tracks in the snow! I followed them into the tangle and found a deer highway—all fresh. Cars crept by within only yards of me. I could see them, but they couldn't see me in the thicket. I began looking for a tree so I could get a few feet off the ground to allow me to look into the thicket. The only tree available was an old cedar. Perfect! The thick boughs would hide me and help protect me from the now minus-seventeen degree wind-chill factor. I clawed my way up, cut a few limbs, and hung my stand. As I sat there I *knew* I would kill a deer. The setup was too perfect. And, besides, anybody crazy enough to be sitting there freezing in the top of a cedar tree within a few yards of a four-lane highway, during the last two hours of deer season *deserved* a deer! Sure enough, within thirty minutes, I caught sight of a big deer with no antlers and a spike ambling calmly toward me. At fifteen yards, I drew and released on the big deer as a trailer truck roared past. I thought its head looked strange, but in the failing light I couldn't tell why. Turns out, he was a big rut-worn buck that had already shed his antlers—and I could tell by the pedicels, they were big antlers! The next day I turned the thicket inside out, but couldn't find the sheds.

That sequence of events tells an important story. Not only do hunters pattern deer, but deer pattern hunters, particularly older deer. That deer "knew" there wouldn't be any hunter stupid enough to hunt that close to a main highway, especially under conditions that miserable. We hunters are pretty predictable when you think about it. We hunt the same places, at the same times, using the same gear the same way—the way the videotapes and magazines tell us to. Only on opening weekend of gun season do we really surprise deer—suddenly invading the woods by the hundreds, after a relatively undisturbed spring and summer. That's why nearly half of all bucks killed during the season are killed on opening weekend. (Plus the fact that the rut causes bucks to lose some of their caution and move more.) That's also why so many green new hunters often kill the biggest deer. The old deer have had enough close calls over the years with seasoned hunters to pattern their behavior. But an inexperienced hunter doesn't necessarily know the ropes—a new hunter is more likely to stumble into the woods at "odd" hours, in "unproductive" spots, using equipment the "wrong" way, etc.

When deer scents first came on the market, they were deadly. But when everybody started using them, they became less productive. New products are always hotter, for a while, until deer pattern them. Deer calls are the same way.

So, what's the bottom line? Dare to be different. If it's a fad, don't do it. Hunt where others don't, when others don't, and how others don't.

A few years ago, a hunter came up after I'd given a deer seminar. A couple of other snickering hunters were with him. He said, "These guys were laughing at my hunting method and I want to see what you think. I hunt a dairy farm and before I get up into my stand, I rub cow manure on my pants and boots." The other two hunters howled in laughter. I asked if he killed deer regularly. "I get two or three nice bucks a year," he responded. I said, "It sounds like a good idea to me! You ought to package that stuff and sell it—but then, after a while, it wouldn't work anymore." The hunter smiled and looked around at the other two. They weren't laughing anymore.

Winter Squirrel Hunting

Well, hunting season's about over. Most of us have cleaned, oiled, and hung up our deer-hunting gear. Relaxing by the fire seems more pressing than brushing icicles out of our whiskers.

But for those of us who have more energy than common sense, there's still some good hunting to be done. I don't know about you, but when I wake up to a sparkling frost or fresh snow on a still, cold morning, my adrenaline starts gushing and common sense flies out the window. My wife just shrugs, shakes her head, and turns back over.

Actually, in most southern states, it's legal to hunt several species in January and February. Some deer hunting is still available, along with rabbit, quail, grouse, and woodcock hunting—to name a few. But one of my favorite late winter sports is squirrel hunting.

Now, there are probably as many ways to squirrel hunt as there are squirrel hunters—well maybe not quite. Basically, though, there's sit-hunting, stand-hunting, still-hunting, stalk-hunting, and dog-hunting. Sit-hunting means to sit in one place on the ground, leaned up against a big tree, and wait. Of course, you need to be situated where squirrels have been feeding. To stand-hunt you wait them out, perched from an elevated deer stand. Still-hunters move slowly through squirrel habitat looking for squirrels, and stalk-hunters creep up on squirrels they've heard barking, jumping, or cutting mast. John Madson wrote that the best squirrel hunter he ever knew "had moss on his north side, a hermit thrush built a nest in his hair, and one day his gunstock sprouted suckers and took root."

I like to squirrel hunt all those ways, but I especially like to hunt with a dog and a couple of friends, including my dad. As with other kinds of squirrel hunting, you need to hit the woods early. But instead of being still and quiet, we laugh and enjoy fellowship together and let the dog find the squirrels.

Now Penny didn't have papers, and she probably had blood from at least a dozen breeds coursing through her veins, but when she barked, you might as well have cocked the hammer. She was one of those rare dogs that could find squirrels with either her eyes, nose, or ears—or all the above.

You can cook squirrels countless ways, and I believe my wife, Daryl, has tried them all. Daryl is a whiz at concocting new game recipes. She prepares most of our game the same way she does domestic meats. I think that's one of the reasons we enjoy it so well at our house.

She came up with another way to prepare squirrel several years ago that I think is outstanding. For many years she has prepared home-made chicken salad. Using this idea, she has found a way to turn a few squirrels into several servings. Here is her squirrel salad recipe:

> Salt and pepper
> 6 average-size squirrels
> Enough water to cover to boil
> 4 eggs, hard-boiled, chopped fine
> 4 ribs celery, chopped fine
> 1 rib sweet pepper, diced fine
> ¼ cup sweet pickle relish, or finely chopped sweet pickle
> 4 Tbs. sweet pickle juice
> ¼ cup mayonnaise
> ½ cup walnuts, chopped coarse

Boil squirrels in large pot in water to cover. Add salt and pepper to taste. Reduce to simmer until meat easily falls away from the bone. (This will vary with the age and tenderness of the squirrels.) Let cool and remove meat from bones. Process meat in a food processor until coarsely chopped (a meat grinder may be used.) Some broth may be used in the food processor, if needed. Add remaining ingredients to chopped meat. Add broth and/or mayonnaise to sandwich spread consistency. Makes about three quarts.

Still sittin' in front of the fire? Didn't think so; good luck. Don't forget to tell your wife (or husband) which direction you're headed. Oh, and be sure to keep your powder dry!

Dressing Smart Helps Whip the Winter Winds

Ever wonder how some hunters can spend hours on a deer stand and not seem to get cold, when other people can just walk outside for a few minutes and freeze? The difference lies in using winter clothes properly. These days, there's no reason people who hunt, ski, or do farm chores in the winter have to be cold. We have so many materials—some old, some new—to keep us warm. It's just a matter of knowing how to use them.

There are different kinds of winter clothing for different purposes. To look at these, let's start next to the body and work our way out. The body tends to sweat with the least bit of activity, especially when you have a lot of clothing on. The layer next to the skin should be made from a material that's thin and designed to transfer (wick) sweat from our bodies through that layer into the next layer of clothing. Often, we get cold from sweat trapped next to our body by a cheap synthetic material. There are different materials that can be used to wick sweat away. A thin layer of wool is good, but some people may be allergic to wool right next to the skin. Silk is also good, but expensive. A thin layer of polypropylene does a super job of wicking sweat away.

If we don't have much clothing on, moisture will go on through the last layer out into the air. But if we have a lot of clothing on, this won't happen. So we need to have a layer to hold the moisture that has been wicked from our skin. Thicker wool is one of the best materials for holding moisture. Even while it has moisture in it, wool will provide good insulation—which brings us to the next layer, the insulation layer.

There are many different kinds of good insulation materials, even though some have drawbacks. Probably the best is camel hair, but it's so expensive it's not feasible. Another one that's very good, but expensive, is angora. Probably the third-best insulation material is wool. Down is one of the best insulators, as long as it's dry, but if it gets wet, it's worse than not having anything on. Another insulator which is often overlooked is air. One kind of insulated underwear has big holes like fishnet. With clothing on both sides of fishnet underwear, the little air pockets that are formed insulate well. Thinsulate is a good insulator; it's light and very thin. It's one of the few synthetic materials that makes a good insulation layer. Depending on how cold it is and how good your clothing is, you may need only one layer of insulation—sometimes two, and occasionally three.

On a windy or rainy day, you'll need an outer layer that repels wind or rain or both. If it's just windy, a nylon windbreaker—very thin, very light—on the outside of all the other layers of clothing works well. On days when it's lightly raining or just foggy, a layer of Gore-Tex is effective. Gore-Tex is a synthetic material, with very tiny pores that allow sweat vapors to escape to the outside, but prevents rain droplets from coming in. Before you buy Gore-Tex though, make sure the Gore-Tex membrane is sandwiched between two layers of good protective material, so the membrane won't be damaged. Also check the seams to make sure they're waterproof. If you're in the rain for a long period, especially if it's raining hard, Gore-Tex won't keep you dry. For these conditions you need a medium to heavy vinyl or rubberized rainsuit with welded seams. For cold, rainy conditions, I recommend wool-insulated gloves.

Be sure to dress in layers. You might start out the day extremely cold in the morning, and get pretty warm by midday. Taking off one piece of heavy clothing when you begin to sweat, and putting it back on when you get cold, is what colds are made of! With layers, you can take off or put on a layer at a time to help you regulate your temperature.

When I was a boy, I stayed cold in the winter. I dressed in layers all right, but all of my clothing was of the same size, and bound me up so tightly I couldn't move. This reduced the blood circulation, especially to my legs and arms, and made me cold. It's a good idea to have your outer clothing a size larger than you normally wear, so it's large enough to go over your other clothing without binding you. For example, I normally wear a size 10 boot, but my insulated pack boot is size 12, so I can have room for a thin pair of wool socks for wicking and a thick wool pair for insulation and to hold the sweat. My feet never get cold now.

Most body heat—as much as 80 percent—is lost through the top of the head, the chest, and the neck area. For that reason, it's very important to cover and insulate these areas well. Believe it or not, this will also help keep your hands and feet warm. I like a down vest, because this allows me to have insulation over my chest without heat buildup in other areas. A down vest is also something you can put in your pocket to put on when you need it most. For the neck area, I like a wool scarf—some people like a turtleneck sweater. Either is fine. For the head area, you need something extremely warm, and I prefer a double-knitted wool pullover cap. I have deer-hunted with one of these caps all day in pouring rain and never had my head get wet—or cold—simply because wool holds moisture and still insulates. There are other suitable kinds of head cover, but remember that your head sweats just like the rest of your body, and wool will allow moisture to escape, keeping your head dry. Have a warm, enjoyable winter!

Part III

Animals Make the Land Interesting

Patterns among Animals

As wildlife biologists, we know through years of study certain principles of wildlife behavior and interaction between wildlife and its habitat. We can predict what will usually happen in certain scenarios. The term "usually" is a key one, though. With nature, we don't deal in absolutes and "always." Wild animals are individuals, and like people they don't always follow the book. Perhaps that's what makes wildlife study so fascinating. In the accounts that follow, some fit the "usual" pattern and some don't.

Dominance in Animals

The scene was both comical and fascinating. After all, it's not every day you see a lizard doing push-ups! But there he was, up and down, up and down, his flattened orange throat sack distended like a vertical leaf. The critter was a green anole, known locally by the name chameleon, because of its ability to change color to match its surroundings. The reason for his antics was obvious—to demonstrate his dominance to another male, crouched low on a stick below him.

Dominance is a "position" within the social structure of a population of animals. Most animal species have a dominance hierarchy, with one or two dominant individuals at the top, one to two at the next level down, and so on. In other words, each animal in the population has its place. If the dominant animal is killed, the next one down quickly assumes the dominant role. The dominant animal is usually the biggest, strongest, and most aggressive.

With some species, it may be the most brightly colored. In polygamous species (in which one male mates several females), the dominant male attracts more females. In monogamous species (in which one male mates one female), the dominant male mates the most attractive female (the one that is healthiest, most youthful, etc.). The advantage of this is obvious. The mating of the best insures that the offspring will be the fittest. They will be most likely to survive the rigors of nature. So the species not only survives with the passing of time, but its genetics keep improving.

The most dominant animal often gets the best food—and more of it, too. A good place to notice this is at the bird feeder. In some species, in addition to a male-dominance hierarchy, there is also a female-dominance hierarchy. A social group of does, for example, usually includes an old doe, her young of the year, her young of last year, their young of the year, her young of two years ago, and so on. In this case, the grand old dame is usually dominant.

Now, when there are two animals at the top with about the same size, strength, and aggressiveness, something has to give. They eventually have to settle the question of who's dominant. And to do that, it often takes a good, old-fashioned, knockdown, drag-out fight—sometimes to the death. On occasion, buck deer have been found, both dead with antlers locked together. In such cases, they usually die of starvation. When I was a student at Auburn, we found a giant old buck that had been killed by a car. He was covered with battle scars, old and new, but what apparently did him in was the blindness in both eyes. One eye was freshly gored by an opponent's antler tine, and the other appeared to be lost through infection, possibly from an earlier fight.

In most cases though, dominance is established without a fight. After all, if you can scare an opponent away, who wants to get bloody? Bucks often establish dominance by late summer or early fall, with shoving and semi-playful sparring bouts. This is much like two boys proving their strength by arm wrestling. Males of some species never touch each other to prove dominance. Some land turtles, for example, settle dominance by height. The one that can hold its head highest earns the privilege of respect. Some have even been seen to stand with their front feet on a small rock to gain a height advantage. All is fair in love and war, I guess.

I attended an interesting seminar a few years ago given by Dr. Susan Riechert, a noted zoologist at the University of Tennessee. For her doctoral dissertation, she had studied dominance behavior in a spider species indigenous to the dry climate of the western United States. She found the spiders occupying webs covering horse tracks, made by a single horse soon after one of the area's infrequent rains. The small depressions were preferred because the area's limited moisture collected on the webs. Insects attracted to the moisture were caught in the webs, making them easy prey for the spiders. She noticed that there were more spiders than suitable web sites (tracks). Challengers would climb onto the web—on the opposite side from the spider occupying the web—and bounce the web a few times. The spider occupying the web would, therefore, bounce a few times too, then one of them would leave. Since spiders have poor eyesight, she theorized that body weight was the factor that determined dominance. To prove this, she flattened small lead shots and glued one to the back of each of several smaller-than-usual spiders. Sure enough, when the weighted-down little spiders bounced, the larger spiders vacated! Just goes to show I guess—perception is at least half reality. My dad always said, "Bullies aren't necessarily tough—they just act that way."

Sex Differences in Animals

Nearly everyone can tell a male cardinal from a female by the bright red plumage. And most people can distinguish a drake mallard from a suzie by his bright green head and white neck band. Bucks have antlers most of the year, but does don't (except in unusual cases). But it's hard to recognize the difference between sexes of many wildlife species.

The Canada goose, woodcock, bluejay, and channel catfish are just a few examples of species with few visual differences between sexes. It usually takes a biologist with some experience to distinguish the sex of these species. (The animals themselves don't seem to have any problem, however.)

And then there are those species that fall in between—ones where the average person can't tell the difference, but if you know what to look for, it's easy. The wild turkey is an example. Males have breast feathers that are black-tipped, while the females' breast feathers are buff-tipped. The mature gobbler has a beard and spurs. The hen doesn't, except in unusual cases.

You can sometimes tell the difference in sex by field sign. Droppings of the gobbler are generally straight, with a bulb on the end, while hen droppings are corkscrew shaped. The placement of urine in relation to tracks in the snow is a sure way to tell a buck from a doe.

Reptiles and amphibians have some interesting differences between sexes, too. The bottom part of the shell of the male eastern box turtle is concave. This helps the male stay on top of the high-domed female during breeding. The male's eyes are red, and the female's are brown. (I don't know what purpose that serves.) The males of some lizard species have a great deal of color on the belly side, while females have little or no color there. During courtship and territorial behavior, the male does what appears to be "push-ups," expanding his sides, making the color show. Males of many frog species have color on the throat that is visible when the air sac is expanded. This is most noticeable when frogs "sing" in the evening and at night to attract mates. Bullfrog males have large, darkened typanic membranes (external eardrums), while those of the female are smaller and lighter colored.

Size differences between sexes vary, too. We normally think of males as being larger, such as is the case with deer, elk, and turkey, but with most reptiles and amphibians the females are larger. This seems to be necessary to allow the females to carry more eggs or young. Most reptiles and amphibians give little or no care to their young. Because many of the young are lost to predation, a large number is necessary for a few to survive.

While we're on the subject of caring for the young, there are some interesting differences here as well. With most species, only the female takes care of the young. But there are some in which the male spends as much time caring for the young as the female. The bobwhite quail is one example, and the mourning dove another. Not only does the mourning dove male care for the young, he is equipped (just like the female) with a gland in the crop that produces "dove milk," a nutritious liquid which is mixed with seed in the crop. The young put their head inside the mouth of either mom or dad and feed vigorously on the contents of the crop.

So, what does all of this have to do with anything? Some of us use our knowledge of species to help manage them. One of the oldest management tools, for many species, is to harvest only one sex—usually the male. These are often polygamous species, such as turkeys, deer, elk, or pheasants. This means that one male will breed several females, so harvesting a certain number of males will not lower reproduction. Of course, when the population gets too large for the habitat, we have to harvest both sexes to adequately lower it. Whenever a species gets into trouble, though, one of the first things a biologist looks at is reproduction. Telling the boys from the girls is helpful.

As for the rest of us? Well, it's nice to understand more about the world we live in. It makes our lives a little richer.

Black and White Animals

(No, not zebras nor skunks—read on!)

As I turned the corner last week, I noticed a student holding up a poster of a black cat to admire. "Great picture," I commented as I walked by. "Yeah," he said, "I love black panthers." Well, I could have kept walking, but I've been an educator too long. I had to stop and tell him it was really a black leopard, not a black panther. I eventually convinced him, but only after finding a reference to back me up. I had to chuckle at his comment (mostly to himself) as he left: "I can't believe I've been worshiping the wrong animal."

Common names vary, depending on who you talk to, but the name panther is most often used for the North American cougar, *Felis concolor*. A black version of this species would be very rare. A black version of the spotted leopard *(Panthera pardus)*, on the other hand, is pretty common in its native habitat—the tropical or semitropical rainforests of Burma, Malaysia, and Thailand.

The black color in animals is caused by a black pigment called melanin. This pigment is usually found in the form of granules, contained in cells known as melanophores. Black animals have an abundance of melanin, grey animals have less, and spotted animals have clumps of melanophores. A black individual of a species not normally black is called a "melanistic" individual. The gene that carries the normal color is dominant and the gene that carries the black color is recessive. That means an animal with both kinds of genes will be normal, and one with only black genes will be black. In practical terms, if a pure spotted leopard (one with only the dominant gene) mates with a pure black leopard, none of the offspring will be black, but all will carry the black genes. If two of these offspring mate, one out of four will be black. If, for some reason, black animals survive better in a particular environment, there will be enough black animals to mate with each other regularly. This will cause the black (melanistic) phase to be more common. In the case of the black leopard, the black color blends in with shadows of the rainforest. They can catch more food because they are better camouflaged, and prey can't see them as well. This process is called selection.

The opposite of melanism is albinism, the absence of melanin. An albino has three distinctive features: 1) white hair, feathers, or scales; 2) reddish-white skin; and 3) pink eyes. The reddish or pink color is caused by tiny blood vessels which show through. In normal animals, they are hidden by pigment.

Albinism is caused by the meeting of two recessive albino genes. The albino gene blocks the production of tyrosinase, which is the first biochemical step in the formation of melanin. Now, just when you think you understand, nature throws you a curve. There are different degrees of albinism—caused by a series of albino genes which control the intensity of color. Some albinos are off-white, and some white on only parts of the body.

Melanin screens light to protect eyes and skin from harmful rays of sunlight. An albino is disadvantaged because it can't usually see as well, it stands out to predators, and it's sometimes not recognized by others of its species.

Albinism occurs in almost every animal group, including man, but rarely. For example, albinism in man appears in only one out of twenty thousand births. In unusual cases though, small populations of albino individuals occur. Kenton, Tennessee (close to where I live), is proud of its population of albino grey squirrels. Don't confuse the name with the color—the species is the grey squirrel *(Sciurus carolinensis)*, but the color is white, snow white. These beautiful creatures live right in the town proper and are vigorously protected by town folk. This is probably the reason the recessive genes have survived. Even though albinos are more vulnerable to predation, predators aren't as abundant in town. Too, once a few build up in number, white becomes their favorite color for a mate.

Most things about nature aren't black or white, but a few are. And when you see one of these rare creatures, enjoy the experience. Most folks are never so fortunate!

Predators Have a Place

One morning, before I had finished my second cup of coffee, I received a typical phone call. An anxious, determined voice on the other end said, "Byford, I've got to get rid of some foxes. Do you know where I can get some strychnine?" The simplest thing would have been to tell him where he could get strychnine. But, being conscientious, and never one to do something the easy way, I told him that poisoning foxes is illegal. Then I asked him why he wanted to get rid of foxes, anyway. He sounded surprised, "You're a wildlife specialist, so you ought to know. They're eating my quail—that's why."

Many hunters believe that game is scarce because there are too many predators. They feel their hunting prospects are reduced by whatever number of animals predators catch. So, by this logic, removing predators would make game more abundant. Sounds logical at first, but let's look a little deeper.

Predation is a natural law in the wild, and nature is like a complicated machine. Not only are all the parts necessary, but so are all the functions. Predation is as necessary as life and birth—its main function is to reduce population surplus. Now, it may be hard for a quail hunter who has flushed only one or two coveys of quail in an all-day hunt to imagine a surplus of game, but most wildlife species are prolific. At the normal breeding rate, one pair of grouse would produce more than 33,000 birds in only 6 years if no losses occurred. One pair of deer would produce more than 3,000 in 20 years. It's been estimated that reproduction from one pair of plant lice would crowd all other living things off the earth in 12 years! Keep in mind that predation is not just the killing of game by predators. The chickadee feeding on plant lice is just as much a predator as the great horned owl killing a grouse.

Predation isn't the only thing that reduces wildlife numbers. If all predators were removed, disease, starvation, parasites, or weather could take up the slack. The number of animals a unit of habitat can support has a limit. This varies with different species and with the quality of habitat, but the fact is, some factor will keep numbers at that limit. This limit is called the "carrying capacity."

Results of a predator control study carried out by the New York Conservation Department many years ago illustrates what may happen. After the near-removal of all predators, a low population of 33 birds in the fall of 1933

Predation is a natural law in the wild, and nature is like a complicated machine. Not only are all the parts necessary, but so are all its functions . . . fooling with the natural order of things is tricky business. An immature great-horned owl.

built up to 87 in the fall of 1943. Although the same intensive control of predators was continued, the population dropped from 87 to 15 between September 1943 and April 1944, apparently as a result of disease. Another example: the natural predators of deer in North America (the wolf and the cougar) have been largely killed out because of people's fear of them. Without predators, a carefully controlled deer harvest is necessary each year to keep deer numbers within the bounds of their habitat. There are several case histories where deer hunting was stopped. In all cases, deer built up to large numbers, overbrowsed their food supply (actually lowering their own carrying capacity), then starved.

The bottom line is that fooling with the natural order of things is tricky business. It seldom works the way we expect it to. If we remove foxes, other predators become more efficient, or other factors come into play to lower numbers. If you don't have many quail, look at the quality of your quail habitat. Predators become discouraged when there's enough cover for the prey to hide in. In good habitat, they will catch the excess, especially the old and sick, but long before they have caught too many, hunting becomes more difficult, and they will shift to other prey species for easy picking. And because they keep the inferior animals cleaned up, we continue to have wildness in nature. The ones strong enough, smart enough, and fit enough do survive and reproduce.

Now all of this is hard to explain on the phone in a couple of minutes. It's especially hard when a gruff voice comes back, "Don't preach to me, I want to know where to get strychnine...."

Tales about Mammals

Deer Do the Strangest Things

I was way down in the riverbottom, about a mile from the nearest road. It was late in the deer season, and I had a doe permit. At 7:05 A.M. I caught the forms of three does easing through the thick brush toward my stand. I picked out the middle-sized doe—plenty of venison, and I judged that the meat would be tender. I picked an opening I thought the does would walk through and cocked the hammer on the old model 94 Winchester. When the third doe reached the opening, I lined up the iron sights and squeezed the trigger. As I fired, all three deer bolted and headed south, across the bottom and uphill toward my truck. I knew I'd made a good hit, but I waited thirty minutes before moving to look for sign. Sure enough, there was a good blood trail, and I found her easily, about sixty yards away—a good lung shot.

After field dressing her and poking around in the rumen to see what she'd been eating, I began the long, tough drag. I'd been dragging for about thirty minutes when I heard a shot from the direction the other two deer had gone—about an hour and a half after I killed this deer. I glimpsed a flash of orange in a thin strip of timber across the large pasture. I watched as the hunter eased out of the timber and began slowly moving toward me. He had his head down—it was obvious he was looking for blood. He began slowly circling, head still down. He stopped, took off his cap, and scratched his head, as if confused. He slowly looked all around, then spotted me. "Hello," he hollered across the field, "would you mind helping me look for my deer?" I yelled back that I would help, then started over to him.

It was a good break. I was tired of dragging anyway. When I reached him, he was excited and confused. He had trailed the deer out into the forty-acre pasture that was heavily grazed and then lost the trail. "The danged-est thing happened," he said, as he began his story. He had gotten a slow start that morning because of car trouble. The sun was well up in the sky (about 8:30) as he was walking across the pasture to his stand. Suddenly, he heard a loud splash, then another, about eighty yards on the other side of a thin fenceline of cedars. He slowly eased up and peered through the cedars and saw two does swimming in a farm pond—in the middle of the pasture. He pointed to the pond, and we both marveled that there was absolutely no cover around it! He was so astonished that he wasn't ready to shoot when the first one reached the bank and climbed out. It walked over the dam out of his sight. But when the second one climbed up on the bank, he fired. He didn't know if he'd made a good hit or not, but he did find blood, about forty yards away as the deer entered the thin strip of timber. After going about fifty yards into the timber, the blood trail led back out into the pasture to the spot we were standing, but he couldn't find any more blood.

After piecing the events together, I told him I thought those two deer were the ones traveling with the one I killed. We both got down on our hands and knees and started looking. Success! I found a spot of blood no larger than a pinhead, then another, and another. We picked it back up as it continued farther out into the wide-open pasture. After about forty more yards I looked up and saw another pond. The trail was headed straight for the pond, at least one hundred yards from the nearest cover. We followed the trail right up to the pond's edge and saw fresh walking tracks in the mud at the pond's edge. The deer had definitely gone into the pond, walking. I said, "OK, let's split up and walk around the pond until we find where she left it." He agreed, and we carefully looked for fresh exiting tracks in the pond's muddy edge. This pond also had no weedy or brushy cover at all.

When we met on the other side of the one-acre pond, we stared at each other in amazement. There were *no tracks* leaving the pond!? We carefully looked out into the pond for the deer but didn't see anything but calm, muddy water. I said, "Let's go back to where she entered and look again, this time even more carefully." As I was studying the tracks entering the shallow water's edge, I noticed something that looked strange. There were two tiny *holes* in the water about four feet out, about the size of soda straws. I was puzzling over that when it hit me. It had to be the deer's nostrils! Suddenly, the deer burst out of the water with such force that he and I jumped back in startled amazement! The deer was swimming frantically. I cautioned him to wait until the deer was near the shore before shooting, or he would have to swim out into the 35-degree water to retrieve her. When she reached the bank, the hunter was so shook up he missed seven times before he finally put her—and him—out of their misery.

We both sat down in total disbelief. In a combined total of fifty years of deer hunting between us, we had never seen a more unusual situation!

Deer Are Meant to Be Wild

Running the risk that I may lose credibility by telling strange deer stories, I've got another one for you. It happened on a cold Saturday morning several years ago, when I lived on a fifty-four-acre farm near Knoxville. Julie, my daughter, had just returned from feeding sheep at the barn. She rushed upstairs, out of breath. "Dad, I just saw a deer in our garden!" Well, that may not seem strange to you, but at that time, we had never seen a deer on our place. They had been restocked about three miles away two years before that, but we had never seen any. We had overnight guests, and we were sitting on the sofa enjoying our morning coffee. "Aw, Julie," I chided, "Wipe the sleep from your eyes, girl— you're seeing things." Everyone laughed—everyone, that is, except Julie. She stomped downstairs, somewhat annoyed. "OK," she said, "Come downstairs and see for yourself. He's in the house now." We all looked at one another, because it's not like Julie to tease. I walked downstairs, puzzled, and Julie was pointing down the hall at the deer, who was cautiously peering out of my son Brad's bedroom! I couldn't believe my eyes. There was a deer—not only on my place, but in my son's bedroom. Julie had been so excited that she had rushed into the house, leaving the sliding-glass door open.

I didn't know what the deer would do next, so I told everyone to stand back, in case the deer decided to bolt out of the house. The deer instead cautiously walked up and smelled my hand! I told Brad to go to the barn and get some sheep feed. While he was gone, the deer let us stroke it on the head. It looked to be a yearling buck that had just shed his antlers. When Brad returned, it eagerly ate the sheep feed from his hand. By the time he had eaten all the sheep feed, all of us had taken our turns at petting the beautiful creature.

Then he began acting strangely— he was interested in Brad; *very* interested! It began following Brad, trying to rear up on his back. Brad, who was twelve at the time, was alarmed and shouted, "Dad, what should I do?" I told him to take off his coveralls. He was wearing the same coveralls he had worn while deer hunting a few months before and while birthing lambs that winter. Apparently the doe scent he had put on while hunting and/or the placenta fluids from the sheep had piqued the young buck's interest.

After we tired of petting the deer, I got an idea. I had built a high-tensile, predator-proof electric sheep fence a few months earlier, and I was curious to see how the deer would react to it. The fence design was similar to that recommended to repel deer from orchards and other high-value crops. I told Brad to put the coveralls back on and entice the deer to follow him down to the fence. Reluctantly he did so, and sure enough the deer readily followed. Brad stopped and stood next to the fence. The deer cautiously walked up to the fence and sniffed it. Zap! What happened next was sort of a blur. The deer turned a somersault, landed on his feet and zoomed across the driveway, right through the fence on the other side! Realizing he was on the wrong side of the fence, the deer pranced excitedly around, his ears laid back. He alternately approached the fence, then retreated several times. He then bolted right through the fence again and disappeared into the woods.

The young buck stayed gone about two hours. When he returned, he buddied up with Brad again, and I asked Brad to repeat the procedure. He gladly followed Brad until he neared the fence. The young buck put on the brakes about fifty feet away, and Brad couldn't coax him any farther, not even with sheep feed. I had learned what I needed to know—the fence worked.

I related the story to a friend of mine who was an outdoor columnist for a Knoxville newspaper. I told him to use the opportunity to tell his readers not to try to tame wildlife. It was obvious to me that the deer had been caught as a fawn and raised in captivity. The fate of such an animal, now grown, would probably not be good. If it survived until hunting season, it probably wouldn't survive long after. An unsuspecting hunter would probably kill the creature before he knew it was tame. My friend Sam printed the article, and I got a call that same afternoon from a neighbor. He confirmed my suspicion. Another neighbor had found the young fawn and had raised it until it became ornery in captivity. He let it go and quit feeding it.

Fawns are seldom orphaned. And even when they are, they can fend for themselves within a few weeks after birth. No doubt about it—deer are meant to be wild.

Status of the Puma, Ghost of the Southeast

"I tell you, I know what I saw." Ed Kendal's dander was up. "I was sittin' on this ridge deer huntin' just before dark. This thing screamed at me—nearly made me swallow my Red Man, it was so close! Just as I turned around, he made two leaps and was gone." Three young men listened with their mouths open and eyes wide, but most of the farmers in Caleb's store were giving Ed the horse laugh.

There's probably more mystique and fear surrounding the puma than any other wild critter in the Southeast. Small wonder. Very, very few people have ever seen one. The puma is known by many names. Its scientific name is *Felis concolor*, but other names include cougar, mountain lion, panther, and catamount. Its range includes most of the United States, just a little of southern Canada, and most of South America. There is only one species, but thirty subspecies.

In all, three kinds of cats roam the woods in the southeastern United States. The most common one, of course, is the house cat, *Felis domesticus*. Don't laugh. A lot of people have seen large house cats in the wild and thought they were pumas. Many a wildlife biologist has driven hundreds of miles to see a dead puma, only to discover, once on the scene, that it was just a house cat. Some feral house cats are just as wild as pumas, too.

The bobcat, known in some areas as the wildcat, is the second kind of cat found in the Southeast. Dubbed *Lynx rufus*, it's much smaller than the puma; large males reach no more than thirty pounds. In many ways, it resembles a large house cat, ranging in color from yellowish-brown to gray, with many black or brown spots and streaks. The biggest difference between the bobcat and the other two is that it has a short "bobbed" tail, from which it gets its name.

Now the puma. The largest male puma on record was eight feet long, three feet of which was the tail, and weighed 260 pounds. But understand that this was the *largest* puma ever recorded. An unusually small specimen, on the other hand, was only four feet long and weighed 46 pounds. Of course, the average-size puma is somewhere in between. The puma, like the house cat, has a long tail. It has short, close fur, which varies from yellow to red, but is usually yellowish-brown. A lot of folks think they're black, but a black puma is probably as rare as a black deer. Basically, in the Southeast, we are dealing with two subspecies—the eastern puma and the Florida puma.

Pumas disappeared from most of the eastern United States soon after settlement. Settlers feared the animals and were reluctant to share their livestock and game with the large predator. They are easily hunted with dogs, so they were quickly decimated. Another factor was that deer, their main food item, were wiped out by the settlers as well. There is concrete evidence that a few cougars survived in the Great Smoky Mountains National Park between 1900 and 1930. But since that time the animals have continued to go downhill.

There have been two major studies during the last two decades on the status of the puma in the southeastern United States. One carried out by Chris Belden and his staff of the Florida Game and Fresh Water Fish Commission examined the Florida puma. The U.S. Fish and Wildlife Service and the U.S. Forest Service jointly sponsored a study of the eastern puma, headed up by Robert L. Downing.

Both teams of researchers had some trying times. Sometimes their job seemed like—well, like looking for ghosts. They got lots of reports. Most of them were misidentifications, though, made by well-meaning folks. Some reports were sightings by other biologists, but the researchers couldn't verify the sightings or find substantial sign. Some reports were really pumas, but they were the western subspecies. Did you know it was possible at one time to buy western pumas from captive stocks in Florida? Indeed, it may still be. (The western puma is plentiful enough that there is a hunting season on them in several western states.) Many people vacationing in Florida could buy one for the novelty of it. As they returned north along I-75, many discovered they had bitten off more than they could chew. By the time the pretty little cat had shredded their back seat to ribbons, they were ready to let it go. And they did—the first time they passed through a large wooded area. So even a field sighting by a biologist is not a verified eastern or Florida puma.

So what is their status? Most biologists would like to believe that eastern pumas still exist, but most will tell you they don't. After his exhausting efforts, Bob Downing could find no concrete proof that they exist. Chris Belden, on the other hand, actually located and radio-collared a few Florida pumas. The species definitely does exist, but the numbers are few. How long it can hold on is still in question.

May the ghost of the woods never completely leave us, because what's a campfire without ghosts? Shhh! I thought I heard one just now—a piercing scream on that ridge behind us! . . . Really!

Mating Ritual of the Grey Squirrel

It was 6:15 A.M. on a cold, clear November day. In fact, it was the day after Thanksgiving. I had just settled into my deer-hunting stand, perched high in a tupelo gum, overlooking a semibrushy riverbottom. A slight movement to the right caught my attention, and I slowly looked around. It was a squirrel; no—two squirrels, three! One was preening itself, but the other two had other things on their minds. One slowly crawled out on a one-inch diameter limb, and the other followed. Carefully and deliberately, the second one eased up to the first, and mounted it. The mating lasted about eight seconds. He dismounted, went under the limb to the front of the female, licked her face, went back and mounted again, this time for about five seconds. He dismounted and slowly the female moved up the tree to another limb stub and sat there, perfectly still, for about fifteen minutes. The male remained on the first limb, humped his back, as if ejaculating again. After about three or four minutes, he slowly descended the tree and started foraging on the ground. Another life cycle begun.

I've spent a lot of time in the woods in the last four-plus decades, and though I had many times seen the courtship chase, this was the first time I had ever witnessed grey squirrels mating. I've since related the incident to several other seasoned hunters, none of whom had ever seen the event. I recall a wildlife professor telling a class many years ago that, after a long, tiring chase of several males following an estrous female, the male with the most stamina eventually mated the female, over and over again, inside a tree captivity. Since the scene I witnessed didn't fit this scenario, I was curious. So I did a little research and here's what I found.

When a male squirrel senses an estrous female (usually in late December), he gives a short, tail-flipping signal, then examines the female. She bounds away, followed by the male in a slow ground chase. As his excitement grows, he begins an odd buzzing deep in his throat. This usually catches the attention of other males in the vicinity, and they join in the chase. The female scrambles up a tree and tries to shake her admirers in a reckless flight through the treetops. She pauses to rest while the excited males sprawl on nearby limbs, waiting. When she is finally cornered by a male, she emits a screaming snarl, and the suitors shrink back, silent and subdued, keeping their distance for several minutes. In subsequent mating attempts by first one male, then another, she each time gives the piercing, hawklike scream and shakes them off.

After an hour or so of frenzied aerial courtship, one male—usually an old, dominant, scarred warlord—leads the pack of suitors. He snarls and slashes at any who try to overtake him. Eventually the other males one by one beat a retreat back to the ground to forage for food. As the female shrieks her repulse, the dominant, usually large, male vents his rage and frustration by tearing away bark with his teeth. Now, the female waits on a limb while the restless male stalks about her, with his tail fluffed and trembling with nervous excitement. His teeth chatter and his forefeet strike the branch. The two squirrels exchange soft murmurings and growling. The male sidles closer with his tail curved forward, slightly to one side, while the female studies him in profile. Eventually, the female gives in and the age-old courtship once again culminates in blissful union.

One researcher reported as many as thirty-four males pursuing one female! Sometimes the ultimate pair stays together for as long as two days, until the female is satisfied and the male is exhausted and happy to go away—to rest up for his next mate.

Though squirrels have been known to breed every month of the year, there are two distinct breeding seasons. There is a light summer breeding period beginning in June, but the main winter breeding season starts in December. The act of breeding I witnessed evidently was one of the first unions of the winter. As far as the mating behavior of my two squirrels, I can only imagine that most of the courtship had already occurred—probably the day before.

I can't imagine how anyone who has spent a few hours on a deer stand thinks of it as boring!

The Opossum: An Unusual but Resilient Mammal

"No, Mr. Hensley, opossums do not breed through the nose." There was a slight pause on the other end of the line, and then he replied, "Are you sure? You see—me and a couple of fellows down here at work have a bet ridin' on this, and we knew we could find out the right answer from the university." Actually, the timing of the call couldn't have been better. Up to that point, I'd had a rough day. I needed a break—something a little less serious. So, I dug out a reference and read these words to him: "Contrary to an old belief, opossums do not mate through the nose. In mating, the penis enters the single opening of the female reproductive tract, the forked ends penetrating the paired vaginal canals leading to the two uteri, or wombs."

Of all the critters we have in the Southeast, the opossum is one of the most unusual. It's the only marsupial in the United States. Members of this group, which include the well-known kangaroo of Australia, carry their young in pouches. The scientific name, *Didelphis*, means "double-womb." The other part of the scientific name, *virginiana*, means "of Virginia," honoring the colony where the mammal was first described. The common name, "opossum," is of Native American origin. In his *History of Virginia*, Capt. John Smith (yes, the one linked with Pocahontas) noted: "An opossum hath a head like a swine, a taile like a rat, and is the bigness of a cat. Under the belly, shee hath a bagge." The language is a little old-fashioned, but pretty descriptive.

The opossum is tough. One reason is that it eats a lot of things. Opossums have sometimes been described as scavengers, because they feed on human garbage and carrion. This merely shows their adaptability, because they'll eat a wide variety of food. They'll eat small ground animals, such as earthworms, grasshoppers, beetles, ants, snails, snakes, and toads, in the summer and fall, together with voles, mice, and small birds anytime. They love eggs, chicken, and other poultry, too. Plants are eaten when animal food is scarce, but they'll take persimmons any time they can get them.

I recall an old saying back home that "possums taste so bad, dogs won't even eat 'em." Actually, several animals eat them, including bobcats, coyotes, foxes, and owls. I like opossum myself if it's fixed right. The secret is to remove the fat. Put the animal on a drip tray in the oven at about 350 degrees and render all the fat out by baking. Once all the fat has melted through the rack into the drip tray, the meat can be taken off the bone, mixed with barbecue sauce, and put back into the oven in a casserole dish. Believe it or not, it's good!

Everybody who has grown up in the country knows that opossums "play 'possum." When the opossum is confronted by a dog and can't escape, it turns at bay, hisses, and growls. If the dog succeeds in grabbing and shaking the animal, it suddenly goes limp and rolls over with its eyes shut and tongue out, as if it had suddenly died. Strangely enough, the dog often loses interest and leaves. A few minutes later, the opossum gradually recovers and runs off. Some have suggested that paralyzing substances are released into the opossum's brain to produce the deathlike state. More recently, though, experiments with "brain wave" machines have shown they are not in a trance or catalepsy, but are wide awake.

Several years ago, a zoo caretaker called my wife, Daryl, and me to ask if we would keep several baby opossums whose mother had died. We agreed. I discovered that their favorite food was chicken bones from table scraps, and their second favorite was persimmons. I was amazed to discover how clean they were. After every meal, they would preen themselves like a cat. They would lick their paws and wash any part of the body their food had touched. They were easy to feed, too, because they would eat about anything. After a few weeks, they grew rapidly. We put them in a larger pen outside and fed them there for a few days. We then opened the top, so they could leave at will—and they did.

Like Rodney Dangerfield, the opossum garners little respect. Most folks think of it as "the ugliest, dumbest, biggest klutz of an animal I've ever seen." Fast as a cheetah—slick as a weasel—or cunning like a fox, the opossum is not, but don't sell it short. We have far more opossums in this world than cheetahs, weasels, or foxes. H'mmm–that's worth thinking about.

Tales about Birds

One of Nature's Spectacles

You know, people spend a lot of money every year trying to break out of the rut of their everyday lives. Everybody needs a little excitement now and then, but it doesn't always have to be expensive. I've had many exciting things happen in my life. One special one I'd like to share with you happened on a warm spring afternoon several years ago. I was hunting turkeys in a west Tennessee riverbottom. The turkey sign wasn't too bad—a little scratching here and there, some hen droppings, some gobbler droppings, and a few wing primaries that had molted out during the winter. I tried hard the evening before to roost a gobbler, but wasn't able to. So, the next morning I went down into that black riverbottom, and, in the shivering cold, I built a blind. At first light, I hooted like a barred owl. Nothing. In a few minutes I hooted again—no response. After about thirty minutes, I decided to move on down the bottom. Later that morning, I finally located one gobbler, but he apparently had several hens and wouldn't work to me.

That afternoon, I decided I would go to the other side of the management area and scout a little more. I parked the truck and headed into the bottom again. After thirty or forty yards, I began to wonder if I ought to look any farther. The riverbottom had been flooded most of the winter, and practically all the vegetation had been destroyed by fast flood waters. However, I almost immediately began to see turkey tracks! After walking a little farther and looking a little closer, I discovered abundant turkey sign in the hard-caked mud. I was easing along when I caught a glimpse of something moving about 150 yards away. I couldn't tell what it was, so I quietly closed the distance. When I got to within about 100 yards, I saw that it was two turkey gobblers fighting! I quickly glanced at my watch as I slowly crouched—three o'clock. It was truly amazing! They backed off about six to eight feet, carefully eyed each other and, lowering their outstretched wings, suddenly clashed wing-to-wing, throwing their spurred feet toward each other's breasts. As their wings hit, they made a loud popping noise. The gladiators would fall to the ground, their heads and necks intertwined, break apart and stagger back, obviously very tired and spent. In a matter of seconds, though, they regained their composure and repeated the same sequence. I watched them do this over and over for about five minutes. And, suddenly, almost as if there were a signal, they broke apart. One left the scene with his head high and chest out; the other left in another direction, with his head lowered submissively. Meanwhile, as I watched all this, I crouched a little closer to the ground every time they hit each other. I looked desper-

The gladiators would fall to the ground, their head and necks intertwined, break apart and stagger back. . . . His dominant genes were the ones that perpetuated the turkey flock, and they're probably still evident in that flock today. Two wild Merriam's turkey gobblers in Nebraska, fighting for dominance.

ately for something to hide behind, but found nothing but a four-inch limb on the ground. I was positioned flat on my belly, nose nearly in the mud, with my shotgun barrel sticking over my limb. As soon as the two turkeys disappeared, I clucked softly with my mouth yelper. No response. After waiting three or four minutes, I yelped softly three times. Off to my left where the subdued turkey had gone, he suddenly appeared, running toward me. As he ran, he nervously looked both right and left, as if trying to approach me unnoticed by the other gobbler. He ran to within ten yards of where I lay, and then suddenly realized he'd made a fatal mistake.

Turkeys, like most other wildlife species, have a pecking order or dominance order. This issue of dominance is usually settled without fighting. But sometimes when two animals are about the same size, they will fight it out. One fight usually is all it takes to put the lesser animal in its place. When the dominant individual is taken out of the system through hunting or predation, the next one will step in to take over.

In the situation of the two gobblers I saw fighting, I killed the lesser gobbler. I don't know what happened to the other gobbler—I never did see him again. Perhaps he was just a little too smart to be fooled by my clumsy clucks and yelps. Whatever the reason, his dominant genes were the ones that perpetuated the turkey flock, and they're probably still evident in that flock today.

I've seen a lot of exciting things over the years in the woods. And to tell you the truth, even though they haven't cost me much, I wouldn't take any amount of money for them.

Crows: A Part of American Farm Life

It was early spring, and I was out at daybreak scouting for turkeys. It was a cold, damp morning, and the overcast sky occasionally showered a light, misty rain. I was in the Obion River bottom in northwest Tennessee, where I had seen some turkeys the previous fall during deer season. I was easing along when a startled hen turkey burst from a treetop over my head, showering me with raindrops and flapping furiously for parts unknown. The critters were quiet—no one gets too peppy on a morning like this. Almost no one. Suddenly, a group of crows about two hundred yards to my left began a noisy ruckus. Crows in the distance from several directions began joining the excitement, and soon the sky was alive with excited, diving crows. I was curious, so I eased over in that direction. Soon I saw the cause for the commotion. A Cooper's hawk was perched in a swamp chestnut oak, and it was forced to duck its head every time a crow dived at it. In the distance another hawk screeched its disapproval, but the crows wouldn't let up. The first hawk flew toward me and perched in a tree over my head. As I looked up at it, I saw the reason the hawks wouldn't leave. There was their nest in a large fork of the tree.

Nobody knows why crows heckle hawks and owls, but it's a common occurrence. A few sharp caws and every crow within hearing distance will descend upon the poor bird. The chase may continue from woodlot to woodlot until the crows grow tired of the sport. It's a strange phenomenon when you consider that the hawk or owl could tear an individual crow apart. I've also seen blackbirds do the same thing to hawks, owls, and even individual crows.

The crow family includes about one hundred species, including ravens, rooks, magpies, and jays. The two crows in the Southeast are the common crow and the fish crow. The fish crow *(Corvus oxifragus)* is found only close to the ocean, but the common crow *(Corvus brachyrhynchos)* is found all over the region.

Crows raise one brood (three to seven young) each year. They start nesting in March, building their nests 20 to 60 feet high, usually in woodlots next to farmland. By mid-April most clutches are complete. They incubate the pale blue to light green eggs for 18 days, and the young fly when they're about 3 weeks old. By July, the young birds start feeding in flocks of 10 to 15. Flocks become bigger as the season advances, and by winter they may contain up to 25, 000 birds (up to 200,000 in some western states). Some crow flocks may migrate south as far as 1,000 miles in the winter (but some migrate 100 miles or less). Once they settle in their winter location, they may forage daily in a 20- to 30-mile radius from their roost.

Crows eat about anything resembling food they can cram into their craws. One old study by the U.S. Fish and Wildlife Service examined 2,118 stomachs of crows from 40 states. The researchers found 650 different food items. Just over one-fourth of the annual diet was animal matter, including insects, spiders, millipedes, crustaceans, snails, reptiles, amphibians, wild birds and their eggs, poultry and their eggs, small mammals, and carrion. Insects made up over two-thirds of the animal matter, and most of them are injurious to agriculture—May beetles, white grubs, wireworms, weevils, grasshoppers, and caterpillars. One stomach contained fragments of 123 grasshoppers, and another the remains of 483 small caterpillars. Nearly three-fourths of the crow's yearly food is vegetable matter, more than half of which is corn. Much of the corn is taken from harvested fields, but as farmers know, crows also pull corn sprouts, damage ripening ears (in the milk stage), and feed on dry corn on the stalk. Crows may also damage other grain, mainly wheat, at sowing or sprouting time.

Only one-third of 1 percent of the crow's yearly diet consists of eggs and nestlings, but crows can be a significant predator to game birds in some situations. In the western states, crows were found to destroy up to 30 percent of the duck nests in one waterfowl concentration area, and up to 12 percent of the pheasant nests in other areas.

All in all, crows are more annoying to farmers than damaging, and in several ways they actually help the farmer. I, for one, think that if crows were gone, I would miss them. I can't imagine watching the sun come up without hearing the cawing of crows in the distance.

Feeding Habits of the Crow

One day I received a letter from John Wiggins of Springfield, Tennessee. John was prompted to write me and relate an incident he had witnessed—something he had never seen in all his years on the farm. He said four crows were milling around in the field he was plowing. He hadn't been paying attention to them until he noticed one running up the furrow toward him on the tractor. About twenty feet from the tractor, the crow flew off with a mouse in its beak. After that, he started noticing the other crows and saw them carrying off at least six more mice in their beaks. He noticed that as they landed in the field, they would chase the mice on the ground and catch them in their beaks. John said that over the years he had seen hawks catch about everything that lives in fields, including mice, rabbits, birds, and even snakes, but he had never seen crows catch mice before. He also found it unusual that they used only their beaks, whereas hawks fly down and catch mice with their feet.

Like John, I had never seen a crow catch a mouse, although I knew that mice have been found in food-habit studies of crows. It prompted me to go to the library and do a little digging. I could only find one reference in the literature about crows eating mice. This study, which had been done in 1918, didn't mention anything about how the mice were caught, but it did identify some mammals that crows eat. Mammal species were determined by sorting through bones, teeth, and fur found in regurgitated pellets (pellets are indigestible parts of food that are regurgitated—by hawks and owls also). Upon examining several hundred pellets from a crow roost, the researcher found the remnants of fish, bones and scales of a snake, four meadow mice, a star-nosed mole, two short-tailed shrews, and large fragments of bone.

Though I didn't find any reference to the way crows feed on mice, I did run into some interesting accounts of how crows feed on other things. There was one account of crows carrying eggs to a location before eating them. At one site the researcher found 37 eider duck eggs and 24 herring gull eggs. In another place he found 22 eider duck eggs and 28 gull eggs. The crows were reported carrying entire eggs in their beaks. At another island, the researcher witnessed eggs being punctured by the crows' beaks on site. Crows have also been seen carrying off down nestlings of ducks and gulls. One person reported seeing 16 young chickens carried away by crows.

In 1905, one observer reported watching crows carry clams, scallops, mussels, and sea urchins to a considerable height and letting them fall on the rocks to be broken. The crows would then swoop down and eat the contents. This habit is shared by other birds, notably herring gulls. One person noted that he saw seven crows taking their turns at the carcass of a dead seal. They have been seen eating worms by thrusting their beak into mud and pulling the worms out, similar to the way robins do it. They have been seen foraging this way on mudflats near the ocean and also in lawns. One researcher noted, after watching crows feed on worms in a lawn, that they would cleanse the worms with their beaks before swallowing them. In 1893 one observer related seeing crows eat twenty good-sized trout that had been hidden in a spring. Years ago, farmers along the Maine coast complained that crows were a nuisance in removing fish placed on their fields as fertilizer. Similar activity had been reported in New Brunswick and Nova Scotia. One worker has seen crows enter the business district of Wichita, Kansas, to feed from garbage pails behind restaurants. Another reported that in Iowa, crows often hang around slaughterhouses to feed on the waste of slaughtered animals. Crows are commonly seen feeding on car-killed animals. One worker in 1884 watched crows feeding on a carcass of a dog while the temperature was 14 degrees below zero.

In closing, I'd like to share a couple of other incidents I found in the literature that I thought were interesting. One was about a farmer in New Jersey who had planted five acres in corn and ten acres in asparagus. He noticed that in the lower end of this field where the crows were present each day during the early morning hours, there was no harvest. He jumped to the conclusion, from published accounts of crow depredation on farm crops, that the birds were responsible for his loss. He declared war on the crows, and left dead ones as a warning to others. After a number of crows were killed, he examined their stomachs and found a mass of greenish liquid filled with cutworm heads, black beetles, and other undigested material. On the following day, he visited the fields about the time the crows were accustomed to being present. He decided not only to let the crows be, but to place ears of corn on the ground to encourage them to come back. They did come back, and they cleared the field of cutworms—thus rewarding the owner with a full yield.

Another experience was related by a farmer in Massachusetts. He owned several acres of pasture where sheep grazed. He felt that the crows were killing some of his newborn lambs, so he declared a bounty, and local hunters killed nearly all the crows in the region. About three years later, he called an agricultural agent to get help in determining what had destroyed the grass in his pastures. The grass had been cut at the root by white grubs, which had increased rapidly after the crows had been killed. The farmer withdrew the bounty, crows returned, and his pastures gradually recovered.

How Birds Help Farmers

Whoever coined the phrase "eats like a bird" should have intended it to mean *eating much and often,* instead of not much at all, as it's usually intended. Birds are hungry most of the time. Their high metabolism and short digestive tract demands they eat a lot often. They not only fill their stomachs with insects or seeds, but also their crop or gullet, if food is available. A study reported in 1913 by the U.S. Bureau of Biological Survey (now the U.S. Fish and Wildlife Service) revealed the astonishing capacity of birds' stomachs. It also shows how indebted farmers are to birds for the destruction of noxious insects and weeds. A summary of some of the results follows:

—There were 100 grasshoppers in the stomach of a Swainson's hawk.
—In the retreat of a pair of barn owls, there were more than 3,000 skulls; 97 percent were mammals—mostly field mice, house mice, and common rats.
—A tree swallow stomach contained 40 entire chinch bugs and fragments of many others—also 10 other species of insects.
—A bank swallow in Texas devoured 68 cotton boll weevils, one of the worst insect pests to ever invade the United States.
—38 cliff swallows consumed an average of 18 boll weevils each.
—Two pine siskin stomachs contained 1,900 black olive scales and 300 plant lice.
—A killdeer stomach taken in Texas in November contained over 300 mosquito larvae.
—A flicker stomach had 28 white grubs.
—A night hawk stomach collected in Kentucky contained 34 May beetles, the adult form of white grubs.
—Another night hawk from New York had eaten 24 clover leaf weevils and 375 ants.
—Still another night hawk had eaten 340 grasshoppers, 55 bugs and beetles, two wasps, and a spider.
—A boat-tailed grackle from Texas had eaten—at one meal—about 100 cotton boll worms, besides a few other insects.
—The investigators finding that tree sparrows each consume one-quarter ounce of weed seed per day estimated that, in an agricultural state like Iowa, tree sparrows annually eat approximately 875 tons of weed seeds.

The many, many species of birds are all especially adapted to feeding in different places—on different kinds of food. For example, trim and agile wrens creep in and out of holes and crevasses hunting for hidden insects. Woodpeckers have strong claws for holding firmly when at work, a chisel-like bill driven by powerful muscles to dig out insects, and a long tongue to further explore hidden retreats of insects. All other birds have similar unique adaptations.

Birds tend to gather in areas with lots of food. They are not likely to destroy many beneficial insects such as the praying mantis and lady bug, because they are seldom abundant enough for the birds to concentrate on. However, crop insect pests, such as boll weevils, cabbage worms, etc., are so abundant they attract many birds which ultimately catch or kill most of them.

Hordes of blackbirds can be a real pain in the farmer's backside—pulling corn sprouts, eating ripening corn, and stealing livestock feed—not to mention using the farmstead for a bathroom. But even they are helpful on their trip back up north in the spring, gleaning fields of insect larvae and weed seeds.

Well, I can understand if you don't put out the welcome mat for blackbirds. Sparrows and pigeons, too. But most of our other feathered friends deserve a tip of the hat. Come to think of it, though, bluejays sometimes get into our pecans, mockingbirds into our cherries. . . .

Hummingbirds

It was 10:00 A.M. and I was intently listening for a late-morning gobble. I thought I heard one on a distant ridge but wasn't sure. I was decked out in full camouflage, including head net and gloves. Buzz–zz-zzrp! Not two inches from my nose, an inquisitive hummingbird was checking me over. After buzzing my face for a few seconds, the jewel-like miracle of nature lit on a tiny limb about eight inches from my face, cocked his head from one side to the other for at least thirty seconds, totally confused as to what I was. If you're one of the folks who wonder why I go tromping in the woods year after year, this is one of many reasons!

Hummingbirds are truly beautiful creatures. While there are 340 species worldwide, only three are found in the southeastern United States. Two of these—the Cuban emerald hummingbird and the rufous hummingbird— are seldom seen, but the ruby-throated hummingbird is fairly common. It weighs about as much as a penny, and the male is distinctive with a fiery red throat, iridescent green back, and forked tail. The female is dull-colored and has a blunt tail with white spots. Immature birds resemble the adult male, but only have a small red dot on the throat.

The hummingbird has amazing flying ability. It can hover, fly forward, backward, or sideways—even upside down! Its wings can beat up to two hundred beats per second in quick maneuvers, and the critter can fly up to sixty miles per hour. Unlike other birds, the wings have power on both the upstroke and downstroke.

Because of their rapid flight, hummingbirds use enormous amounts of energy and must refuel continuously. Sugar is their energy source, derived from nectar of the one to two thousand flowers they visit daily. They supplement this sugar diet with proteins and vitamins from tiny spiders, aphids, and other small insects. To store enough food for their nonstop flight across the Gulf of Mexico, they double their weight just before migration. On cool nights when the hummingbird's body can't maintain an active body temperature, or when it can't get enough food, the bird goes into a dormant state called torpor. The body temperature drops, its breathing and heart rate are reduced, and the bird's body uses only one-twentieth the amount of energy needed during normal sleep.

Hummingbirds winter from Florida, south to north-central Mexico, to Costa Rica. They nest in the United States in spring and summer. Their nesting activity is located around abundant nectar-producing flowers and a good water supply. They prefer wetlands, moist ravines, and wooded streams, and are commonly found feeding on buttonbush and jewelweed in the bottoms.

The male usually precedes the female in migration to nesting grounds. When the female arrives, the male courts her by rising high in the air, swooping past the female within inches, and rising again on the other side. He resembles a jeweled pendulum, rising back and forth in front of the female, sunlight flashing on his iridescent feathers. After mating, the male flies off to mate with other females, leaving domestic duties to her. She carefully constructs a walnut-size nest (usually near water) from moss, bud scales, and plant fibers—lined with fine plant down and camouflaged with lichens. The nest is woven together and fastened to the limb with spiders' silk. When it's finished, it often looks like a knot on a branch.

The female lays two tiny pure white eggs and incubates them for about two weeks. She often lays a second clutch before the first brood leaves the nest. Young hummingbird chicks, no bigger than bumblebees when they hatch, stay in the nest from ten to thirty days, depending on how often they're fed. The female feeds her chicks entirely on insects she has digested in her crop. She inserts her long bill deep into the chicks' bills and pumps nourishment into them by regurgitation.

If you want to attract hummingbirds, you need two things—food and water. If you have a stream, small pond, or wetland nearby, you're set on water. If not, a small pool or birdbath may work. For food, you can go two ways—plant large, colorful flowers or provide artificial feeders filled with colored sugar water. Gardens and planters filled with fuchsia, sages, bee balm, impatiens, cypress vine, trumpet creeper, Rose of Sharon shrubs, mimosa trees, hollyhocks, and other plants with red, tubular flowers are very attractive to hummingbirds. In fact, more than 160 native North American plants depend exclusively on hummingbirds for pollination, because the long floral tubes with nectaries at the end can't be reached by most insects.

Sugar water feeders supplement the hummingbird's natural diet. Fill feeders with a boiled solution of one part sugar to four parts water, dyed red with food coloring. Don't use honey or artificial sweeteners, and keep feeders free of mold and mildew. Placing an artificial red flower around the feeder tube may attract the birds initially.

There's no reason not to leave feeders out all year. They won't keep birds from migrating when they need to, and may help some birds survive during times of food scarcity—especially ones that migrate late or arrive early. Go ahead and enjoy hummingbirds—they're truly one of God's little miracles!

Snipe Hunting

It's almost a lost art now, but when I was a boy, "snipe hunting" was a popular form of recreation. The men would usually introduce the sport to the boys. The boys, in turn, couldn't wait to take girls snipe hunting. It was especially fun at parties. It was also fun for the country boys to take their city cousins, whether the cousins were boys or girls.

I'm sure most of you have been snipe hunting, but in case you haven't, here's how it works. The best time to hunt snipe is after dark. Any night will work, but dark nights are best. Because, you see, snipe are secretive and shy, and it's hard to get them stirred up and moving in the light. It takes two kinds of people to hunt snipe—the drivers and the catchers. The drivers are the folks who've been before, because they know how to stir them up. The catchers are the folks who haven't been before. That's just how it is, that's why. Now, the catchers each have to carry a burlap bag (we used to call them "tow sacks"), and each has to wait along a trail by him or herself. The drivers stir them up and drive them to the catchers, and the catchers catch them in the bag. When you catch one, you quickly close the bag and tie it up. Catchers are supposed to stay put until the drivers come back to get them. Got it? What? What do snipe look like? Well, they're kind of hard to describe—sort of small and furry. OK? Let's go.

Now, when all the catchers are put out, each quite a distance from the others, the drivers go back to the camp and giggle for a while (the length of time depends on their age). When the drivers have had all the fun they can have, and the catchers are about as scared as they can be, the drivers go back for the catchers, and they all have a good laugh (the drivers that is). I understand some catchers have been left out all night. Maybe that's why some folks are scared of the dark!

I learned about snipe hunting when I was very young, but I was in college before I learned that there is such a thing as a real snipe! And it's a game bird that you can really hunt—with a shotgun, not a sack. Today as I speak to folks about wildlife, I'm amazed how many refuse to believe that snipe really exist. It seems that the longer they were left "holding the bag," the harder it is for them to believe.

The Wilson's snipe is a migratory game bird closely related to the American woodcock. Its legs are a little longer, and it is more streamlined. It's about ten and one-half inches long, and it has a long bill that measures two and one-half inches. The brown plumage is barred with black, which makes it appear to have horizontal stripes. It has a black crown and black stripes through the eyes, and is mostly whitish underneath. Like the woodcock, the snipe can easily open its long bill at the end while probing the entire bill length in soft mud. This helps it eat earthworms (its main food) and other small critters, such as insects and snails. Snipe keep to the cover of vegetation and are most active in the evening or early morning.

Because of its preferred foods and method of feeding, snipe like moist habitat—usually in open country. Marshes, bogs, riverbanks, and damp meadows are typical habitats. In farm country, they can often be found in wet portions of pastures.

During courtship, the snipe flies to a considerable height, then dives rapidly with tail spread and wings half-closed and beating slowly. This results in a soft, resonant drumming sound as the bird glides and soars. The drumming is produced by air hitting the very rigid outer tail feathers whose vanes are held together by an unusually large number of hooklets. The feathers vibrate rapidly to produce a humming note, and the tremulous effect is added by air being pulsed by the slowly beating wings.

Snipe nest on the ground in a grass-lined hollow in a clump of vegetation. Three to four eggs are incubated for nineteen to twenty days, and the young leave the nest shortly after the down has dried. Like killdeer, adult snipe run to and fro, displaying to attract predators away from the young. The young, meanwhile, dive head first into the course grass to hide. The young are fed by both parents and fly when two weeks old.

Snipe hunting—real snipe hunting—is done with a shotgun. And hitting one is about as hard as hitting a bat with a bow and arrow. When flushed, they fly up on rapidly whirring wings and zig-zag before darting away. The alarm call they give as they flee is a harsh grating or a rapid squeaking "ship-per" or "chip-per." Some say it's nothing more than a horse laugh at the frustrated hunter!

So the next time you're invited to go on a snipe hunt, squint your eyes and ask, "Day time or night?"

The Amazing Woodcock

Did you ever hunt woodcock? Tricky, to be sure—with or without a dog. They usually sit tight until you nearly step on them. When they finally flush, your heart turns inside-out and skips about two beats while they hastily wing their departure, zig-zagging among the trees. It's about like trying to hit a dove darting in seven directions at once—and on top of that, you don't get to see them coming.

The opportunity to hunt this sporting bird is getting rarer every year though. Declines are a result of the changing American landscape, a product of our changing lifestyle. Suburbs, mini-farms, and mature woods have replaced the farm fields and young growth forests that woodcocks need.

The woodcock flourished in the first half of the twentieth century as people migrated to cities, leaving abandoned fields to grow up into young woods. Today many of these woods and fields have been developed. Much of the remaining woodland has matured and no longer provides the mixture of clearing, brush, and young woods where woodcock once thrived. In other words, woodcock habitat has dwindled because much of the land is no longer managed for agriculture, wildlife, or timber. Also, success in controlling forest fires has resulted in fewer openings for new forest growth.

The woodcock is a strange bird! Believed to have once been a shore bird, it has evolved some unique features to help it adapt to life in the woods. Its eyes are located far back on its head to allow vision for a full 360 degrees. Its wings are short and rounded to help it maneuver through dense cover. Its long, flexible bill is designed for probing soft soil for earthworms, its favorite food. Perhaps the most unique feature of all is that the woodcock's brain is upside-down! The woodcock is well camouflaged in the leaves and remains motionless until flushed. But believe you me, when it finally takes off, it is anything but motionless.

The mating flight is truly spectacular, as well as strange. At dusk or dawn (or all night if the moon is full), the male soars two hundred to three hundred feet upward in a spiraling flight, then plummets in a zigzag fashion back to the ground. This is followed by a ground display to impress the shy watching fe male. This ritual is performed in a clearing known as a "singing ground."

Though most woodcocks breed in the northern United States and Canada, some breed in parts of the South. In the fall they migrate southward, individually (not in flocks). They wait for favorable winds, because they can't fly well for long distances. They winter along the Atlantic Coastal Plain and in southern bottomland hardwood swamps, with Louisiana holding the largest number of wintering birds. Their wintering habitat is dwindling, as is their breeding habitat.

Woodcock numbers can be increased through simple habitat-management techniques. They need several habitat types. Because they nest in shallow depressions on the ground (often at the base of a tree), they need young, open woodlands for nesting. They need dense thickets with moist soil for daytime feeding, and clearings for courtship flights. One helpful technique is to clearcut small strips through mature woods, then cut a new strip next to an old one every few years. This technique, which provides a continuous succession of young growth, also benefits a number of other wildlife species. Before beginning management, you need to carefully inventory desirable habitat types already present, either on your land or on adjacent land. It may be desirable to leave certain areas undisturbed. Foresters and extension agents and specialists can help you with management. We can bring this great little bird back. We know how—we just need to do it!

Vultures Are Interesting Creatures

A few years ago, Dad and I were building a tractor shed when I looked up to see a large black bird next to my pickup. As I approached closer, I could see it was a black vulture. I expected it to fly away at any minute, but I came within five yards before it began to walk away. I followed as it began hopping out across the pasture. I chased it to the pasture's edge where it jumped up on a log, vomited, hopped off the log, down a bank, and was gone. (Vomiting is a normal reaction of vultures when they're upset.) I could tell the bird was injured in some way, but I'm still not sure exactly how.

A few days later, a good friend of mine, Billy Minser from Knoxville, Tennessee, stopped by to say hello. As I was showing Billy my place, I saw the bird about eighty yards away and told him I'd seen it a few days before, and that it appeared to be injured. Billy's daughter Bethany, ten years old at the time, was visiting as well, and Billy wanted to catch the bird and show it to her. We teamed up on the bird and chased it for about a hundred yards before we eventually caught it. I can tell you right now, I have a healthy appreciation for that large meat-tearing beak. The bird swiveled its long serpentine neck around and took two healthy chunks out of my hand before I realized a different holding position on the bird was definitely in order!

Vultures are interesting birds. The two we have in the southeastern United States—the black vulture, *Corheyps atratus*, and the turkey vulture, *Cathartes aura*—both belong to the family *Cathartidae*, the family of New World vultures. The black vulture has a large black beak and a solid black head. Its large wingspan is tipped on each end by silverish primaries. The turkey vulture, also known as the buzzard, has a six-foot wingspan and weighs about three pounds. Its plumage is blackish brown with a greenish gloss on the body. The head is naked and red (brownish in young birds).

The turkey vulture is found in many types of habitat—from forests to deserts, and to the high plateau of the Andes. In some parts of its range it migrates, and in other parts it doesn't. They are excellent fliers, gliding for long distances without flapping their large wings. This is also called soaring on thermals. They've been estimated to fly at forty miles per hour when migrating. Turkey vultures roost in trees and leave the roost only when the ground is warm enough for the air currents to rise, helping them take off. They may perch all day during rainy weather.

Turkey vultures feed mainly on carrion, either fresh or in advanced stages of decomposition. Since the turkey vulture has a smaller bill than the black vulture, it prefers rotten carcasses or those that have already been opened. They feed readily on animals killed by cars, but also catch small live animals, such as mice. They occasionally take eggs and nestlings of other birds—and also have been known to feed on rotten pumpkins and other fruit.

There's been controversy for over a hundred years about the way turkey vultures find their food. Some early researchers came to the conclusion that turkey vultures can't smell. To prove this, Audubon, for instance, covered a carcass with canvas and found that vultures were not attracted to it, but when he placed a picture of a dissected sheep on the canvas, they were attracted. Another researcher covered a putrid carcass with canvass and then scattered meat on top of it. The turkey vultures came to the meat and ate it, but didn't detect the decaying meat only a few inches away. However, recent experiments have shown that turkey vultures will gather at hidden carcasses. It's been found that these birds have relatively large centers of smell in the brain and that they do partially find their food by smell. Further, engineers have noticed that turkey vultures sometimes gather over leaks in gas pipes, where they are apparently attracted by a nasty smell.

During the early part of the breeding season, small groups of turkey vultures have been seen performing a strange dance. About a half dozen birds gather in a clearing and hop after each other, with wings outstretched. One bird hops after a second, which chases a third, and so on, until they're moving in a circle. This dance apparently precedes mating. After mating, two white eggs are laid on the floor of a cave, in a cranny, in a hollow tree, or on the ground in a thicket. Both parents incubate the eggs for about thirty-eight to forty-one days, and the young hatchlings are able to fly when they're about eleven weeks old.

The turkey vulture's greatest enemy is human beings, sometimes by accident, but often by deliberate shooting. They are federally protected in the

United States, however, and it's illegal to shoot them. It's quite possible that the injured bird that I described had been shot. They're often hit by cars while feeding on animal carcasses in the roadway. Turkey vultures sometimes feed on young livestock, but because their bill is so small, they often can't do much harm to a large, living animal, unless it is very weak or trapped. The black vulture, on the other hand, is another story. Its large beak can do quite a bit of damage on a fairly large animal.

Turkey vultures can spread diseases such as anthrax, which they pick up on their feet and heads from carcasses. They are, however, unlikely to transfer these germs to living animals. It is interesting that turkey vultures are immune to the deadly botulinus toxin, which is a hazard to most carrion eaters.

Bird Migration: Much Is Still a Mystery

Have you ever wondered about the miracle of migration? Why do they do it? How do they find their way—there, then back? Several kinds of animals migrate, but birds are best known for traveling long distances to satisfy their needs at different times of the year. Bird bodies are built for migration. Wings, tails, hollow bones, and internal air sacs all help them fly efficiently for long distances.

Humans first recorded bird migration over three thousand years ago, during the times of Homer and Aristotle. Actually, Aristotle believed that birds hibernated in the winter, and this superstition persisted for over two thousand years. In 1703, one observer boldly theorized that birds flew to the moon where they spent the winter. Others ventured that small birds "hitchhiked rides" from large birds. Now we know better—but we're still learning. The U.S. Fish and Wildlife Service has been studying bird migration for more than three-quarters of a century.

So how much do we know about it? First of all, we know that some birds don't migrate. And for the ones that do, a combination of factors gives birds the disposition to migrate. Examples of such conditions include day length, weather, and, in some instances, food availability. But research has shown that the stimulus for migration is too complicated to be attributed to any one of these factors alone.

We often think of birds going south for the winter and north for the summer. There are variations here, too. Some species begin migration in July, while others begin late into the winter. While some migrants are still traveling south, some early spring migrants begin returning north—through the same locality—often leaving plentiful food supplies to go where food is more scarce.

All birds of a species don't migrate at the same time either. In some species the migration lasts so long that the first arrivals in the southern part of the breeding range will have finished raising their young, and may actually start south, while others of the same species are still on their way north. This reflects the fact that northern and southern populations of the same species sometimes exist, and they have quite different migration schedules.

The time of day that most birds migrate is fascinating. Even though most birds appear to be creatures of daylight, many choose nighttime for extended travel. One obvious advantage of this is safety. Another is that, since they use enormous amounts of energy flying, they can alternately feed and rest during the day. Most birds aren't equipped to feed at night.

Large birds fly faster than small ones. Ducks and geese can fly 40 to 50 miles per hour, while some of the flycatchers fly at only 10 to 17. Most birds have two extremes in flying speed, a slow one for ordinary purposes and an accelerated speed for escape or pursuit. Often the reserve speed is as much as double the normal rate. A peregrine falcon would have a hard time catching a pigeon during a level chase at 60 miles per hour. But it can probably exceed 200 miles per hour during a swoop from a great height—to catch its prey. Migration speeds for birds usually fall between cruising speeds and escape speeds.

Birds migrate at several different altitudes, but 95 percent of all migration occurs at less than 10,000 feet. The bulk of migratory flight occurs under 3,000 feet. Geese have been seen flying over 29,000 feet, though, honking all the while. At 20,000 feet a human being has a hard time talking—running or other rapid movement is out of the question.

We still don't know how birds navigate. There have been many theories, but no proof. We do know that they will return to the same area where they were hatched, and if they live long enough, to the same area where they spent the winter the year before. And these areas, in the case of Arctic terns, may be as much as 11,000 miles apart! Unbelievable! What's even more amazing is that they often travel during rain and fog.

Scientists are learning more about migration every day, but much of it is still a mystery. But that's OK. Some of God's miracles may never be completely understood.

Let's Hear It for the Owls

You know, some of my fondest memories include relaxing around a hunting campfire, watching the stars twinkle, and listening to the barred owls on distant ridges, with their "who cooks-who cooks-who cooks for you-awwl?" Owls have different effects on different people. I remember years ago my mother being afraid to hear a screech owl at night, because their weird, bone-chilling call reminded her of someone in distress. It also shakes some folks up to have a large owl quietly wing its way past. Because their feathers are adapted to be quiet, they can fly to within five feet of your head before you know they're around.

There are a lot of myths about owls. Some people think they can turn their head completely around. Not so—they can turn it just three-quarters of the way. They can't move their eyes from side-to-side, but have a flexible neck that allows them to move their heads rather quickly; thus, the illusion of a complete turn. Some people think owls are blind during the daytime. That's not true either, because owls can see perfectly well during the day—even though they can see better at night. All birds are known for their keen eyesight. Owls are certainly no exception, but on top of that, owls have the best hearing of all birds. Their ears are found on the sides of their head and are hidden by feathers. The so-called "ear tufts" on top of the head of some species are really feathers, and have nothing to do with their ears at all.

Most owls hunt at night and are seldom seen by people. They can live their entire lives close to people without people ever knowing they're around. I'm lucky enough to have a breeding pair of great horned owls on my land. This is the largest owl species in the southeastern United States. It stands nearly two feet tall and has a wingspan of nearly five feet. It has large feather tufts on each side of the head and a white collar around its throat. Its song is rather soft, but deep-pitched, and goes something like this: "hoo-hoohoo-hoo-hoo." The great horned owl is primarily a woodland species, but it is sometimes found in parks and orchards.

I also have on my place two or three pairs of screech owls, the smallest of the southeastern owls. They are no more than seven to ten inches tall and have a wingspan of one and a half to two feet. There are two color phases of the screech owl, gray and red. Like the great horned owl, they also have ear tufts. The name screech owl is misleading, because rather than a screech, its call is a plaintive, mellow trill. Research at the University of Tennessee a few years ago showed that screech owls nest more commonly in subdivisions than in deep woods and are readily attracted to nest boxes. It's easy to understand why they like subdivisions better than woods when you realize their food includes a variety of things that live in open areas, such as insects and rodents.

Many farmers are accustomed to seeing barn owls nesting in their silos or barns. Barn owls, which are endangered in some states, consume large numbers of rodents that are usually found around barns and similar buildings. Remains of nearly three thousand mice and rats were found near the nest of one pair of barn owls several years ago. The owl's digestive system breaks down the nutritious parts of the prey, but the indigestible parts, such as hair, bones, claws, teeth, etc., are regurgitated in the form of pellets. These pellets, found at roosting sites, can be checked to determine the owl's diet.

The other common owl species in the southeastern United States is the barred owl. The second-largest owl, it stands nearly two feet tall and has a wingspan of three to four feet. Unlike the larger great horned owl, it has no ear tufts and brown eyes (the great horned owl has yellow eyes). The barred owl is only found in deep woods, and it has the loudest call of all our southeastern owls.

On those nights when you're out camping in your favorite deer or turkey woods, you'll likely hear the barred owl's raucous call in the distance. And when you do—for those of you who know and understand the barred owl—there'll be a peace that comes over you. Because you'll know there are still a few wild places left, like the days of our forebears—days of the buckskins, long rifles, and coonskin caps.

Part IV

Understanding the Land

Through the Eyes of Children

I've said it before, and it bears saying again—adults are much harder to teach than children. Children are like a sponge, soaking up information, both good and bad. They are naturally inquisitive, and don't have their heads so full of misinformation that they can't learn. They're not pressured to make a living, or climb a career ladder, so they have time to learn. They're learning machines—the only trick is to find the right switch to turn them on. The natural world is one of those switches, as long as they can see, smell, hear, or touch it.

Early Years

Love is seldom spontaneous. Instead it grows like the hour hand of a clock, slowly but surely. Love grows over time only after familiarity and intimacy. Unfortunately, some folks never allow themselves to get close enough to the land to know it—to love it. Fortunately, my bond with the land began at an early age.

My first memory of nature is forever etched in my gray matter, as a beautiful bright little bird of deep blue with a sweet high-pitched song. When I was an infant, too young to crawl, Mom would place me on a homemade quilt pallet at the end of the cotton row she was chopping. (For folks from other parts, chopping means hoeing weeds.) The shade of elderberry, pokeweed, and wild plum growing along the creekbank kept me cool, and the beautiful indigo bunting with its sweet song kept me enchanted for hours. It would flit about,

Children are learning machines—the only trick is to find the right switch to turn them on. The natural world is that switch, as long as they can see, smell, hear, or touch it. Trellis Marr, a young 4-H member from Memphis, Tennessee, examining a bird nest in the late 1970s.

catch insects, carry them to the nest, and feed its young. Little did it know the impact it was making on this helpless, small human creature. To this day, of all the beautiful birds throughout the world, the tiny indigo bunting is my favorite. In the natural world, it was my first love.

Growing up in the country, I was constantly surrounded by the beauty of nature. Though economically poor, this barefoot country boy was truly blessed with the richness of a family's love and the splendor of the natural world. Dad held down three jobs—one was farming, one was a 2 to 10 P.M. shift at a local cotton mill, and he was a carpenter on the side. During the summer, Dad, Mom, and I would work the crop. After dinner (what we called the noon meal), Dad would give me a few chores to do for the afternoon. As clear as day I can remember him saying, "Son, if you stay at it, you'll have time to play when you're through. But if you mess around, you won't." Well, you can believe that's where I learned my work ethic, and how to work efficiently. The amount of work he gave me was about right. If I put myself to the task, I could finish in one or two hours—then have the rest of the long summer afternoon for adventure. Dad has only an eighth-grade education, but he has the kind of wisdom you can't get in school.

One of the places I always headed after my chores were done, was the "jungle" I mentioned earlier in the "Wild Enough for Bobcats" piece in Part I. It didn't matter who held the deed to the jungle, it was mine. (At the time, I didn't know about deeds and such things.) It was vast, full of honeysuckle and cedars, oaks and hickories. It had a little stream through the middle that murmured and gurgled as I dangled my stained leathered feet in it, while watching wrens and cardinals carry on without notice of me. And I had secret hideouts and trails through the tangled, viny maze. It was a beautiful place, with shade or warmth, whichever I needed at a particular time. Returning as a man, I realized just how "vast" the "jungle" really was—a woodlot of ten or so acres!

Another one of my favorite places was a pine thicket on a hillside, once gullied but now recovered, protected by the pines. I liked this place in winter, when I would build a warm cozy "den" at the head of a gullied ditch by covering it with old cast limbs and pine needles. There was an abandoned hog pen out behind the barn, with ten-foot-high ragweeds a full inch thick, growing in the black, fertile soil. You could make neat hideouts there where no one could ever find you.

And then there was the "monster gully" back in Uncle Ernest's field. It was at least forty feet deep at the deepest part, and wide enough to hide two eighteen-wheelers—end to end. Somehow as a youngster I knew something wrong had happened that caused the gully, but I couldn't help being fascinated by all the neat sandstones and clays I found in its walls.

Some folks say that growing up as an only child is not good—that it causes the child to be selfish and spoiled. I really can't say since I'm not a sociologist, and I didn't grow up with brothers and sisters to compare. But I know I had a good childhood. Some folks also say that it's not good to let kids pout when they're upset. Maybe for some pouting is not good, but for me it was.

When I felt wronged by someone or by life in general, I would head to one of my natural hideouts where nobody could find me. My parents accepted this and didn't come looking. They knew I'd be back in a few hours. Arriving at my special place of solitude, my mind would be consumed by my trouble. But after a few minutes, I would become enthralled by some natural phenomenon—a hawk catching and consuming a mouse, a butterfly dancing in a sunbeam, or an ant carrying a burden twice as big as it was. In no time my burden was gone, and my heart was light as a feather. My heart was so full of joy, there was no room for trouble nor hate.

I think it was in these sessions with nature that my bond with the land was formed. As the years have passed, I've come to realize that I have two mothers, a natural mother and an earth mother. Just as my natural mother gave me life, shelter, warmth, food, and love, so has and does my earth mother. Just as I ran as a child to my natural mother when I was in pain, so do I now escape to my earth mother when I'm troubled and need peace and solitude. Just as I now feel a need to visit my natural mother, so do I periodically need to visit my earth mother. This is how I keep my life stable—this is one of the key reasons I'm a happy man. This is one of my main weapons against stress.

One of the great sadnesses of my life is knowing there are many folks who have never known their earth mother. She has provided food, clothing, shelter, water, and air—all the things they need to survive. But they have never known the love, peace, and joy that only comes from an intimate relationship with her. And as the generations go by and this society gets further and further away from the land, fewer and fewer of us know her less and less.

Keeping Wild Animals as Pets

Wildlife attracts kids—that's all there is to it. Always has and probably always will. The quickest way to make a hit with a group of kids is to pull out a raccoon, mouse, or snake, and you have an audience. And the generation gap doesn't matter, either. There seems to be a fascination about the way they eat, breathe, crawl, walk, or fly. For some of us, that intrigue never goes away.

Fascination with wild animals naturally leads youngsters to want to keep them as pets. I recall every wild critter I ever had as a pet. I once had a litter of baby opossums that had been left orphaned after their mother was hit by a car. Their favorite foods were persimmons and fried chicken. One pet was a cotton rat I'd caught in a live trap in the shed. After "convincing" my mother that I wouldn't let it out of the cage, she reluctantly let me bring it into the house. I didn't "let" it out, either. Didn't have to—it got out on its own. I never saw it again, but we found signs of it everywhere, including stuffing pulled out of the sofa, droppings in the pantry, and chewed cereal boxes. Mom never seemed to understand that it had to eat, too, same as we did!

I had baby rabbits, a squirrel, and several box turtles. My mother nearly fainted once when I took my straw hat off to reveal a toad sitting on top of my head. Some of my pets died, because I didn't know how to care for them. With others, I managed to stumble onto the right combination of feeding and housing until either I got tired of them and turned them loose, or they escaped on their own.

A lot of folks are tempted to adopt cute and cuddly wildlife babies as pets, mistakenly thinking they are abandoned. Most wild babies, however, are not abandoned at all; their mothers are usually in nearby cover watching your encounter with their young. When we keep wild animals in captivity, we can't possibly take as good care of them as the parents could. Also, many species of wildlife, once they are grown, become either dangerous or destructive. Captive white-tailed bucks have even been known to kill their keepers when they become frustrated—usually during the breeding season. (There's such a story in the March 1988 issue of *Outdoor Life* magazine.) For these reasons, in most states, it is illegal to keep wild animals in captivity without a proper permit from the county wildlife officer. These permits are seldom given, except for educational purposes occasionally.

One animal legal to keep is a pigeon. Pigeons are considered feral and are not protected by law (in most states). Yet, pigeons are fairly common and do quite well in and out of the wild. When I was a youngster, I took a squab (young pigeon) out of a nest located in my neighbor's barn. The squab was in the late pin-feather stage, just about one to two weeks before being able to fly. I kept the young bird in a cage with Mom's setting hens for about three weeks, feeding him hen scratch (a mixture of cracked corn, wheat, millet, etc.), along with a protein supplement. He soon became imprinted on me and quite tame. One day I released him, and after circling the house two or three times he alighted on my shoulder. I fed him and watered him outside with the chickens, and he would land on my shoulder or arm every time I went out of the house. "Pigie" must have thought he was a chicken, because he roosted with them, ate with them, and "talked" with them. He continued to be a pet until he was killed by a predator about three years later.

So, if you or your youngster want a wildlife pet, try a pigeon. They make good pets and are perfectly legal (in most states). Even starlings and English sparrows are legal as pets in most states. They are fairly hardy and easy to keep, and you might find them interesting.

Take a Child Fishing: There's No Higher Priority

You remember the first fish you ever caught? I sure do. I can't say it was much for size, but it was probably the best fish I ever set a hook into. It was a husky four-ounce male bluegill, slightly dark as males tend to be, with a bright orange belly. Many a fish have gone through my creel since then, but none bit so hard, fought so well, or tasted so good as that chunky little bluegill.

It was one of those muggy July days when little boys with pole in hand beg their dads to go fishing. The first lesson I learned that day was that *persistence* pays. After about the umpteenth time, Dad finally agreed. After a few minutes of digging worms around the barn (I loved it!) and finding a pork 'n' beans can to put them in, we were on our way. I remember well the short (it seemed long then) walk down the railroad track. Dad walked on the crossties, but I managed to walk most of the way balanced on a rail. Once we got to the river, Dad thoughtfully studied the situation, showed me how to bait my hook, and told me to drop it down under the shade of that old river birch. You know, the sight of that red and white cork disappearing into the muddy waters of the Forked Deer River is still as vivid to me as if it were happening right now. Dad was as excited as I was, but he tried not to show it. Triumph! First fish on the stringer. I wore his scales off before the day was over, pulling him up to look—just one more time. I wanted to move to another spot so I could catch another fish. Second lesson: *patience.* "Son, when you catch one, stay put; there's probably more." I stayed and caught several more fish, just as Dad said I would.

Well, all of that was over forty years ago. Such a simple outing set a couple of solid foundation blocks in my personality, character, love for the outdoors, and love for my dad. It only took about half a day of Dad's time, but to a little boy, that's an eternity, enough for a true adventure!

When was the last time you looked at your world through a child's eyes? It's really very easy. To them the world is simple, beautiful, and adventure lurks around every bend in the river. The problem with us adults is that we allow our past experiences to limit our expectations of the future. Huh? OK, let's say it another way: children dream and we don't. Children have another advantage over us adults. They have their priorities straight! If they want to spend thirty minutes watching a spider build a web, they do it. We adults let the world go right on by us, while we busily create our own stress.

When was the last time you took a child fishing? Do it! I guarantee they'll be ready to go. Keep it simple and you'll both enjoy it. Let your mind drift with the river. And who knows what influence such an outing will have? There's no higher priority.

Take a Child Hunting during the Holidays

"There he is, son—can't you see him?" "No, Dad, I hear him chewing, but . . ." About that time the squirrel dropped its last piece of hickory nut and ran out the limb to get another one. "Now . . . wait 'til he stops, take careful aim and shoot!" My heart was stampeding, and I could feel the pulse in my temples. A trophy buck wouldn't have made me more excited. The squirrel returned to the same spot on the limb, and I saw him this time. I took careful aim with my .410 and fired; it fell—but hung onto a limb on the way down. I quickly reloaded, but Dad put his hand on my shoulder. "Wait son, he'll fall. You'll someday want to know that you killed your first squirrel with one shot." About that time the squirrel fell to the ground, stone dead. That happened forty-four years ago, but I still remember all the details about that Saturday morning hunt in the little woodlot behind Eldad Church.

When I was a child, families spent lots of time together. There was no TV back then. We worked together, went to town together, played games together, and sat out on the front porch together in the evening, waving and speaking to neighbors passing by. Our music was a natural symphony of crickets, bullfrogs, whippoorwills, and barred owls. I learned a lot by listening to my parents' stories and occasionally stories of neighbors who stopped by. I especially loved the hunting stories. I thought I would burst before I got old enough to go hunting with Dad. And when that Saturday morning came, it was just as grand as I thought it would be. Dad made sure of that. He had scouted the little woodlot and knew exactly where to take me to wait.

After that first hunt, Dad and I hunted when we could. Because he worked three different jobs, he didn't have a lot of free time. But we almost always hunted on Thanksgiving, Christmas, and New Year. While most people had turkey and trimmings and pumpkin pie for Thanksgiving, Dad and I had a bologna sandwich and a ten-cent Baby Ruth candy bar. (In those days, the ten-cent bar was the big one—you could almost make a meal of one alone.) On Christmas day, Dad and I would fill our hunting coat pockets with nuts, raisins, and candy that Santa had brought me. We'd load the beagles in Dad's '52 Chevy pickup and head for the bottoms. It didn't take much to build memories.

Holidays are a great time for parents or grandparents to take a youngster hunting. School is out, and most workplaces are closed. This is quality time. No rushing to meet deadlines, no TV or phone calls to interrupt, no agenda for the day—just a chance to share time with each other and build relationships. If you take a youngster out during the holidays, though, do a little planning beforehand. It doesn't take much to have a successful hunt, but if you don't have some key ingredients, it can be anything from a poor experience to a fiasco!

The ingredients are simple: talk it up, stay warm, don't rush, and don't stay too long. It would help if the youngster harvested a little game, but this is not necessary.

Talk it up. One of the fun parts of any adventure is to talk about it beforehand. Youngsters have vivid imaginations, and they can visualize everything you say. They can see themselves as little David Crocketts in coonskin caps and leather jackets in the uncharted wilderness. But, above all, don't promise heaping game bags!

Stay warm. One of the most miserable times I can remember was on a cold, clammy Thanksgiving rabbit hunt. Three pairs of socks stuffed into rubber boots that were too small for my rapidly growing little feet cut off circulation, and—well, you can guess the rest. You know what it takes to keep you warm. Plan ahead to keep the youngster warm with the same kind of clothes. Pay special attention to warm feet, hands, head, and chest. For feet, I suggest pac boots (with a rubber sole, leather upper, and a heavy wool liner) about two sizes larger than normal, and a heavy pair of wool socks. For hands, good wool or Thinsulate gloves; for the head, a heavy (two layers preferably) wool pullover cap; and for the chest, a down vest under a good coat. A good set of body thermals is a must. Be sure all clothes are roomy enough to prevent cutting off circulation. Because youngsters grow rapidly at this stage, this may mean a new outfit every year or so, but staying warm is critical to the success of the experience.

Don't rush. It's better to get there late than to rush. We rush kids their whole lives. For these special occasions, let the pace be more relaxed.

Don't stay too long. Remember, you're teaching youngsters to hunt. After they have been a few times and have had a few successes, they will be as dedicated as you are and will want to stay as long (maybe longer). But not at first. Remember also that you have more endurance.

Harvesting game is not critical to a good hunt, but a little success just flavors the experience. A bit of scouting beforehand will help here. It also helps to take the youngster shooting a few times before the hunt, so he or she is familiar with the gun and knows how to operate it.

So have special holidays this year. Take a youngster hunting. And keep this in mind: it doesn't take much to build memories!

How the Land Works

The land is complex. The more I learn about it, the more I realize just how complex it truly is. But if you back far enough away from its intricacies, you can begin to see patterns emerge—dependable patterns, ones that make sense and can be counted on year after year, season after season, circumstance after circumstance. And it's comforting to know that the natural world is predictable, even if our often chaotic human society isn't.

Lessons I've Learned from Nature

I've never stopped learning, and I hope I never will. Learning is easy. All it takes is putting yourself in a challenging situation and keeping your eyes open—oh—and you have to keep an open mind, too. My favorite classroom is the outdoors, and my favorite teacher is nature. I'd like to share with you some of nature's lessons I've learned over the years.

Lesson One. Nature can be gentle one moment and powerful the next. There's nothing more gentle than a snowflake falling when there's no wind. The dainty, geometrically perfect ice crystal is as fragile as anything I know, yet it can gently settle to the ground in perfect form. Some seeds, adorned with down-like fiber, parachute to the ground the same way. Mist gently rising from a beaver pond on a cool October morning, while multicolored leaves sashay downward, reminds me how glad I am to be alive.

A hurricane, on the other hand, is probably one of the most powerful of nature's dramas. Tornadoes, volcano eruptions, and floods also fall in the powerful category. Nothing ever devised by humans even comes close, except for the atomic bomb, a case where people have learned to harness nature's power to destroy.

Lesson Two. All things must die so others might live. It's a given. Every living thing will eventually die. And when it does, something else is given life. Some animals are killed so predators can keep living. And if prey are lucky enough to escape, they eventually die anyway. And when they do, their bodies feed scavengers and decomposers—then the remaining nutrients feed plants, which give their lives to plant-eating animals. And if not, they eventually die, too—their nutrients feeding more plants. Sound gruesome? Not really—actually it's comforting to know that I can give something back to the land someday. After all, it's taken care of me all these years.

Lesson Three. Nature gives to us, and it takes away. If we're wise, we'll prepare ourselves accordingly. The same things we depend on to live can kill us if we're careless. Air, for example, is our most frequently needed resource, yet if we fail to heed nature's warnings, it can kill us—in the form of hurricanes and tornadoes. Water, our second most frequently needed resource, can drown us in seconds if we're careless around large amounts of it. Fire is

All things die so others might live. It's a given. Fungi growing from nutrients provided by a decaying log.

a valuable resource for us if we keep it under control—disastrous otherwise. Even food can kill us indirectly if we don't eat wisely.

Lesson Four. Some things are always the same; some always different. We who use the land regularly learn to depend on those things that are always the same. The sun *always* rises in the east and sets in the west. The north star is *always* the first bright star in line with the two stars that make up the front edge of the large dipper. The large dipper *always* revolves around the north star as if it were an axle. Water *always* flows downhill, and so on. On the other hand, some things are always different. For example, the leaves on a tree: even though they were all born from the same seed, each leaf is a little (or maybe a lot) different from all the others. Everyone's fingerprints are different from everyone else's. Every buck's antlers are different—even different sets of an individual buck's antlers are different from year to year.

Lesson Five. Nature, in the broad sense, follows certain patterns. To most folk, nature appears haphazard, sometimes even chaotic. This impression results from infrequent visits to the outdoors. Nature's patterns, though, begin to unfold the more a person spends time afield. But you have to be observant, and you have to take mental notes. For example, cooler weather usually follows wet weather. In our part of the world, south slopes are drier and warmer, because they get more sunlight; north slopes are more moist and cooler. The vegetation reflects that, too. Larger trees and lusher ground cover are found on the north slopes. Higher elevations and rocky soils have clearer streams for obvious reasons. I can almost plan my deer hunt by looking at maps. Topo maps show saddles, ridge clusters, and other topographic features that seem to funnel deer through an area. Aerial photographs reveal islands and travel lanes of cover which also attract deer. Cold-water stream eddies, where the water swirls, tend to concentrate aquatic insects and other food. And you come to expect that if you gently drop the right kind of fly into the eddy behind that big boulder—in the right way, at the right time of day—you may as well get braced for a heart-stopping swirl from a nice trout. In slightly warmer streams, you can expect to find smallmouth bass there.

When the land is cleared, it gradually reverts back to climax vegetation, in a definite progressive order. One example of such a sequence is the succession of weeds to shrubs to young trees to older trees to oak-hickory forest. This is called plant succession, and the trained eye can look at a piece of land and fairly accurately estimate when it was cleared. There are many more patterns in nature, but you get the idea.

Lesson Six. God is alive. I don't believe it's possible to spend much time outdoors without believing in a supreme being. Nature has a definite order, and this order is certainly not the work of people. A classic example of this order is the procreation of a species. Each newborn animal or plant is usually very similar to its parents—definitely not the work of humans, and definitely not a symptom of chaos in the natural world. Scientists have been able to put the ingredients of living things into a test tube, but have never been able to create the "spark" of life. In fact, the more science I learn, the more I realize just how comprehensive, how complex, and how wonderful the natural world really is! I'm still learning, and I hope I always will.

Life Processes Are Not Simple

One trap we often fall into is trying to pinpoint direct cause-and-effect relationships. If the cow gets out, we try to find the hole in the fence so we can fix it. We try to get rid of things that cause us harm and things that don't seem to be of use to us. Truth is, the world is not that simple. John Muir once said that everything in the universe is hooked to everything else. Farming is like that. Farming is the management of a multitude of life processes—and one way or

The more I study conservation, the more amazed I am at how inter-connected and complex life's processes are—and the more awed I become at the wonders of the Creator's work on this land. It doesn't take much intelligence to realize that we'd better not tinker with things we don't understand. Spider web with an early morning dew.

another, all these are hooked together, in a complex way. Science is just scratching the surface on learning how these relationships work.

Oh sure, some things are well known, just not often thought about. For example, we know our crops depend on the pollinators, like honeybees. Without them, we wouldn't have any crops. Yet, how many farmers think about that, or manage *for* honeybees? It just happens. Crop pest predators (predacious insects, birds, mammals, etc.) are essential to crop production. Yet, we continually destroy field borders, the habitat where they live. Thanks to nature's tenacity, there's enough left out there for us to cripple along. The good Lord has been kind enough to forgive us and allow us to make a living. But it seems to get harder every year.

I've been connected with the conservation field for over thirty years. The more I study conservation, the more amazed I am at how interconnected and complex life's processes are—and the more awed I become at the wonders of the Creator's work on this land. It's true that we're making new discoveries every day, but we probably never will understand more than just a smidgen. It doesn't take much intelligence to realize that we'd better not tinker with things we don't understand. The farmer is a land manager, just like the forester or wildlife manager. A wise land manager is one who delicately manipulates the resources to create conditions to favor what he or she is managing for. A wise land manager is never one who wipes the slate clean, and then tries to rebuild from scratch.

ALL THINGS ARE CONNECTED

It was a hot June afternoon, but the clouds were blackening by the second, and a cool north wind was refreshing in my face. As I stepped up on the front porch, a cat scurried underneath. The farmer's wife came to the door and told me I could find her husband over in the east pasture. He was trying to drive a cow to the barn so he could treat her for pinkeye. I thanked her and trotted down to the pasture to help him. He was definitely going to need some help to get her put up before the rain set in. Soon I saw him with another man and a boy trying to drive the cow into the little hay-storage barn in the middle of the pasture. I pitched in and soon we had her inside, cornered her, put a halter on, and tied her to a post. The farmer sprayed the contents of the aerosol can directly into both eyes. As we released her, she trotted out into the now pouring rain.

As we sat down on the bales of straw to catch our breath, I glanced around at the little barn. It had hay stored on both sides and in the loft overhead. There was a breezeway right down the middle, and we could look out to see the rain falling in sheets. There's something I've always enjoyed about sitting on hay inside a good dry barn with the rain pounding down outside.

I knew the farmer, and he introduced me to his neighbor and the boy, the son of another neighbor down the road. The boy looked to be about twelve or thirteen years old. We three men were talking, when suddenly we heard a loud thud. We looked around to see the boy with a stick in his hand stomping something on the ground. A barn swallow was flitting about, darting and diving, then flew out into the rain. "It's them old things again," the boy declared. "Seems I have to knock some down and kill 'em every other week." I walked over to see the nestlings bashed into the ground. I've seen many things die in my time, but this made me sick to my stomach. I looked to see what the farmer and his neighbor were going to say, but they just turned around and resumed their discussion.

On the one hand, I was shocked and saddened—on the other, I understood. I, too, like the young boy, had grown up in an unenlightened environment—a setting where people nurtured the plants and animals that fed them, but paid little attention to most other forms of life. In my boyhood, birds and snakes were killed for recreation and, in the case of snakes, for defense, too. We didn't see anything wrong with it, because everybody in the community did it. As far as we knew, all snakes would either kill you or at least make you sick. I was twenty-three years old before I learned differently. I must have been about eleven or twelve before I began to question killing songbirds for no good reason. I remember the turning point for me. I had just killed a beautiful bird with my BB gun, and as it lay on the ground, I had a sudden rush of sadness and shame, the burden of which didn't leave me for some time. I vowed never again to take the life of any animal without a good reason.

As I matured to manhood, I became an educator and, among other things, have dedicated my career to making others aware of the interrelatedness of all life on this planet. Whether or not we understand it, every piece of nature's puzzle has a function. Killing animals is necessary for other animals to live—this is part of the natural order. And humans are the ultimate predators. But like other predators, people have the responsibility to harvest only those things they use. Game and fish laws are set up so we can harvest the annual surplus, while allowing sufficient numbers to remain unmolested through the reproductive season. Most animals not used for food and clothing are totally protected year-round.

There is irony in the boy's killing of the barn swallows. There's a good chance those barn swallows flitting around the farmer's barn, if left alone, may have cleared up the pinkeye in his cattle herd. It's well known that face flies transmit the pinkeye virus, which sometimes causes blindness in cattle. No recent studies have been made of barn swallow food habits, but an old 1913 study by the USDA reported that insects taken on the wing make up nearly all the diet of barn swallows. And more than one-third of the diet consisted of flies!

Happily, as I travel about and work with youth, I'm finding that today's young folks are more aware. Most of them seem to understand that all natural things on the planet are interconnected and have a purpose—whether or not we understand it.

The Good, the Bad, and the Ugly

I've lectured on many topics during my decades in education. But I guess my favorite topic is "Which living things are good, and which are bad?" I usually open my lecture with that question. Take a brief minute—right now—and ask yourself. The answers are interesting. The first few (after the audience overcomes the shock of such a dumb question) usually get near unanimous support from the audience. Snakes are bad; everybody knows that. Mice, roaches, termites, dandelions—"Wait," somebody says, "you can make some pretty good wine from dandelions." "Yeah," says someone else, "I like the leaves for a salad." "But they're weeds," insists someone else. Youngsters in the room usually sit there with their mouths open, waiting for a fight. But if they knew what dandelions were, they'd probably get into the ruckus, too. Everyone in the room who hasn't blown the dainty, feathery seeds from the round, ping-pong-ball-like head, please stand up. Ummm. Could it be there's some good in weeds? "Nope," someone says, "weeds are weeds, and that's that!" Just goes to show, you can't convince everybody.

What is a weed? Let's go to *Webster's*—everybody else does. "Weed" is defined as "1) any undesired, uncultivated plant that grows in profusion so as to crowd out a desired crop, etc.; 2) . . . a cigar; 3) something useless." Well, I guess *Webster's* agrees that a weed is a weed. If you refer to a basic college agricultural text, though, you'll probably get another definition: weed—a plant growing in a place it's not wanted.

Truth is, different people look at things differently, because they see from different perspectives. A homeowner with a well-manicured lawn sees a dandelion in his or her lawn as a weed. A sightseer may think a yellow blanket of dandelion blossoms covering an April meadow is a beautiful sight. Matter of fact, that same homeowner might think so, too, if he or she sees that perspective. I think a lone cow grazing peacefully on lush pasture in the last rays of the evening sun is beautiful, but when that cow gets into my garden, grazes some of my green beans, and tramps down the rest, I see red. Take Dexter, my daughter's cat. He was the cutest thing since Garfield. But when he turned over a coal scuttle full of ashes, trying to use the bathroom, well—I rest my case.

Deer provide a good example of the good and the bad. Hunters like them, because most hunters aren't around them much until deer season. Farmers are annoyed, though, when they become plentiful enough to destroy their crops in the summer. Most folks—even farmers—like to see deer, especially little fawns with their big brown eyes, in wild settings where they don't cause damage.

While we're on that subject, I've noticed that folks key in on eyes. anything with big brown eyes is cute. Anything with small ("beady") eyes is ugly. Right? Owls, cute. Hawks, ugly. Raccoons, cute. Snakes, ugly. Flying squirrels, cute. Mice, ugly. Big eyes seem trustworthy. Small beady eyes are not to be trusted. Heaven help the person with small eyes. He spends his whole life trying to prove he didn't do it, while the guy with big dark eyes can walk away with the bank, and no one notices.

Back to weeds. If you think about it, most of our weeds are native plants, while most of our crops were originally imported from some other country. Did that ever strike you as odd? The plants we cultivate are selected because

We're all different, but no less—or more—important. The older I get, the more I realize that everything has its place, whether or not we understand it. A black rat snake I kept for over eleven years to teach kids. He was affectionately named "Charlie" by 4-H'ers.

they produce a lot of food that we eat or fiber that we use. And we have to grow crops to produce enough food and fiber to feed and clothe the world. The reason we have to keep fighting the native plants, though, is because they evolved here. Through eons of natural selection, they are best adapted to the soil and climate here. What if we could capitalize on all those years of nature's trial and error and find ways to capture the gene pool from some of those native plants for food and fiber?

I'll stop before the people in the white lab coats come to take me away. But think about it. The good, the bad, and the ugly—an interesting concept, isn't it? I saw a sign one time that said "God don't make no junk." That's true with people and it's true with plants and animals. We're all different, but no less—nor more—important. And, you know, the older I get, the more I realize that everything has its place, whether or not we understand it.

Survival of the Fittest: It's All in the Plan

It's true. This is a remarkable age we live in. We can change our environment to suit our needs more than any species on this planet. We have accumulated so much knowledge, and now have computer capability to store and retrieve that knowledge at will. We can program computers to map out strategies or plans to live by, work by, and create by. We know so much and have come so far. But we sometimes forget that the natural world runs by another plan—one beyond our control.

Several years ago, while sipping my favorite cup of coffee (my first for the day) and glancing down the headlines of the morning paper, my eye grabbed one—"Ice Kills Vast Numbers of Tennessee Trees." Reading on, I noted the author's concern about folks losing money, but more concern for the environment—what it would look like after all those trees were destroyed by ice. If you're concerned, too, take heart. It's not as bad as it seems! First thing is, trees bent over by ice are not necessarily going to die. In fact, one study found that unless the tree is root-sprung (that is, the roots are out of the ground) or the trunk broken, chances are it will live. And as soon as the ice is gone and the ground refirms, the tree will probably straighten back up. But what if the tree does die? And what if its neighbor dies? There are going to be some trees that don't die—and those trees will be stronger. They'll be the ones to produce the seed to continue that species. When you think about it, that's what survival of the fittest is all about, and has been for eons. That's why trees living today have a stronger genetic stock than any that have ever lived. OK, there are some weak ones still living, too, but if they're weak enough, chances are they won't survive long enough to reproduce. The same is true of wild animals. The ones that are tough enough make it through the cold, hard winter when food and cover are scarce. The few left after disease runs rampant—those are the ones that carry on the gene pool. These survivors make the out-of-doors wilder, stronger, and better. Most people have heard of "survival of the fittest," but forget it from time to time. "What's the freeze going to do to the wildflowers?" "What's the freeze going to do to the insects—and the poor birds, how are they going to survive?" Well, many won't, but that's the way the good Lord planned it.

Our society is so accustomed to helping the needy among people that we frequently forget and transpose these values onto wild things. The fact is, millions and millions of plants and animals die every hour. We don't see it, but it happens. Predators kill to eat, often causing their prey to suffer. They're simply surviving. If there's one lesson to be learned in nature, it's that for one animal or plant to survive, another has to die. Are predators bad? Should they feel guilty for killing prey they eat? Predators were made with teeth and curved beaks to tear meat, claws to catch and kill prey, strong jaw muscles to crunch bones, and a digestive system to handle meat and not plants. The same power that made cute rabbits and birds made the predators that kill them. And the plan calls for only the strongest, fittest, and wildest rabbits and birds to survive. I'm not in a position to judge, but if I were, I'd say it's a pretty good plan!

The Effect of Day Length on Nature

I don't know about where you live, but in Tennessee where I hang my hat, we sure have had some mild winters in recent years. With temperatures in the seventies, occasionally I have had to get out my calendar to make sure it was still officially winter. You know it's an unusual winter when spring sales on winter clothes begin in early January.

Some say it's due to the "greenhouse effect"—some say it's normal to have such a warm winter every few years. Regardless, it sure seems strange to run in shorts and T-shirt in January, and to have so much firewood left by early February.

What's the effect of all this warm weather on nature? Will all the plants start growing and freeze with a late winter cold snap? Will insects, ticks, and spiders emerge and be killed? Will birds and mammals start mating and the young freeze? Well, with a cold spell, some of these things will happen to some degree-but it's not that simple. The life processes of nature never are.

First of all, temperature is not the only thing that triggers nature to change with the seasons. Photoperiodism probably plays as much of a role as temperature (if not more). Photoperiodism means the effect of changing day length on life processes of animals and plants. It was first discovered in 1920 and 1923 by two researchers named Garner and Allard. They found that, although many plants were not sensitive to day length, others would begin to flower when exposed to days shorter than a certain critical length (short-day plants). They found that other species (long-day plants) began to flower when exposed to days longer than a critical length, or even to continuous light. They also discovered that yellow poplar trees would grow continuously for eighteen months on artificially extended days in the greenhouse, but some species would not respond this way. Researchers have also discovered that day-length requirements vary within a given species, depending on latitude and altitude.

Later, other researchers found that many species of animals respond to changing day length. In fact, chickens lay more on "long days" caused by extended light. And photoperiodic breeders, such as sheep and deer, will breed at odd seasons when "day length" is changed with artificial light. Apparently, the way changing day length affects animals is something like this. The amount of light in a day travels through the eyes and is detected by the pineal gland of the brain, sometimes called the "third eye" of the animal. At the appropriate day length, this gland reacts by secreting a hormone called melatonin, which stimulates the pituitary gland (the master gland of the body). The pituitary produces luteinizing hormone, which stimulates the testes (obviously in the case of males) to secrete testosterone, and this triggers all sorts of crazy hormone reactions in the body—and the result is increased sexual activity. A similar thing happens in females, except estrogen from the ovary gets things rolling, instead of testosterone from the testes.

Are you still with me? OK. What all this means is that nature is kind of complicated. For some species, warm winters make a difference. For others, they make none at all. For still others, temperature and day length work together to make changes happen. Migration in birds is one natural phenomenon that can't completely be explained by either temperature or day length. Researchers are still working on that one. Even though deer get frisky when a cold snap occurs near the breeding season, temperature doesn't determine the onset of the rut. Day length alone seems to. Deer also get frisky after a weather front moves through following several days of rain—also after the first snow.

So, when you're in the barber shop, and all the local chatter gets around to the effect of warm winters, just remember—nature is complicated! We keep trying, but we'll never understand it all.

Ah, the Woods: What Would We Do without Them?

I'm a creature of the out-of-doors. It doesn't much matter what kind of habitat I'm in—as long as I'm out in the natural world, I'm happy. But I guess if I had to pick a favorite habitat to spend time in, it would be the woods.

Several years ago, I built my own house at the edge of the woods, backed up against the north slope of Bay's Mountain. One of my favorite things to do on Sunday morning is to sit out on my deck and listen to the sounds of the woods, absorb their green beauty, and share in the peace and contentment that comes from things being in order and in place. There's a lot of spiritual enrichment that comes from absorbing the woods.

The woods is made up of many different things, including soil, water, wildlife, shrubs, grasses, and forbs, but the main ingredient in the woods is trees. Trees do a lot of things for us. We all know they provide timber, other wood products, shade, and homes for wildlife. But there are many other things trees provide that we don't think much about. For example, they provide a buffer for sound. Trees protect us from the noises of our human culture, by buffering and muffling sound to soothe our eardrums. One of the most important things trees do is purify the air we breathe.

Trees have a tremendous capacity for filtering out pollutants from the air. But even more important, they produce (as a byproduct of photosynthesis) the oxygen we breathe. Other plants do this, too. But trees have so much foliage that they produce oxygen all the way from ground level to one hundred feet high or more.

Trees help reduce soil erosion, and they have a lot to do with the water we drink, too—something not many folks take the time to think about. See the next section, "Water, the Blood of Life."

As I sit here this Sunday morning and watch the gentle breezes through the leaves, I am truly thankful for the woods and our trees. The more I learn about them, the more I appreciate them.

Water, the Blood of Life

This morning I'm sitting in my study, looking out through the screen door at the rain. It's not a thunderstorm, nor a drizzle—just a steady, wonderful life-giving rain. You know, to me, rain is like a campfire. I'm mesmerized and comforted by its steady rhythm, and I'm awed by its power. I suspect there's some connection between rain and the comfort we felt in our mother's womb. We were cushioned, protected, and comforted by the fluids that surrounded us. And we were warm and comfortable from the heat of our mother's body—much like from a campfire.

Like fire, water can take life or it can save it. Every spring, we hear about life-threatening floods—in the summer, about drownings. Often in the summer, we also hear worried officials talking about drought and water shortages. A few years ago my mother was near death because too much water in her body was crowding her heart and filling her lungs. After doctors removed seven liters of fluid in eighteen hours, she nearly died again from low blood pressure. A sudden infusion of water in her veins once again saved her life.

As we all know, water pollution is a problem in many areas. Lakes, rivers, and underground aquifers are the victims of our carelessness, our ignorance, and our apathy. Fortunately for us, nature recycles our water and cleanses it for us.

It all starts with the rain. What happens when it hits the earth depends on what people have done to the surface. It rapidly runs off concrete and asphalt into sewers, streams, rivers, lakes, and finally the ocean. If the land is bare, eroded silt is swept along, and it drops out at the first point where the water slows down. Rain falling on such unvegetated land results in floods. And if people have invaded the floodplain, extensive damage and lost lives result.

Vegetation on the land allows the rain to slowly soak into the ground, filtering down through organic matter, roots, and rocks. It ends up in underground storage tanks (aquifers) and streams. Many of these underground streams later surface as springs and artesian wells. The amount of vegetation determines how effective the natural filtering system is—forests being best of all. The tree canopy slows down the rain's impact on the soft, spongy forest floor, which is a good biofilter in itself. Of course, water exposed to sun and wind eventually evaporates, escaping to the atmosphere where it forms clouds to later rain again.

Yes, we have a wonderful system. Water keeps us alive, helps us grow the plants and animals we eat, flushes out and carries off our wastes, and gives us recreation. We mess it up, and nature cleanses it. We use it up, and nature replaces it. It's truly a renewable natural resource. Our greatest problem results when we use water faster than the cycle replaces it, or when we pollute it faster than nature cleanses it.

Folks often comment about how interesting some critter is, such as a little bird or a squirrel. I think they're interesting too, but I find folks about as interesting. Seems they're always fretting about something they have absolutely no control over—rain, for example. Some want it to rain, others don't. The conclusion is obvious: if it doesn't rain, we're in trouble! And as far as when it rains—well, we're not in charge of that concern. I'm really glad we're not, too—otherwise we'd have to double taxes to pay for agencies to regulate it, and courts to settle squabbles about it. In reality, we only have two choices about rain: to enjoy rain when it comes or to fret about it. I choose to enjoy it. In fact, I like walking in the rain. Sometimes, when the weather's not too cold, I savor it without umbrella nor raincoat—just me and the rain.

Part V

Taking Care of the Land

STEWARDSHIP

Well, it didn't rain today—first day in a while without rain. The ground is still wet, though, from almost constant rain this spring. It's the middle of May as I'm writing this, and I still don't have that little patch of corn planted—the one I've planned mostly for deer, with a little for me and my wife. While a few farmers have theirs planted, many still don't. And for those whose livelihood depends on farming, the situation has almost become critical.

Rain—when it falls and how much falls—is one of those things out of our control. The good Lord is in charge of rain, and I'm sure He knows best. One of the things we are in control of, however, is our stewardship of the land. As I write this, I'm sitting in a swing which hangs from an old oak which has to be at least 150, maybe 200, years old. The crickets, toads, and whippoorwills are singing, while the fireflies blink their ancient courtship ritual. As I gaze out across the land, I'm struck by the changes this old oak has lived through. Its birth may go back into the 1700s, and its ancestors have come and gone. They dropped the acorns that fed the deer that the Native Americans harvested to feed themselves. And while the old oaks are gone, along with most of the Native Americans, the land that supported them is still the same. The same land feeds us today. The Native Americans didn't own it then, and we don't own it now—not really. They just used it for a while, much the same as we are using it now. Each Native American only had to feed himself and his family, while each farmer today has to feed not only himself, but 134 other people around the world as well. How many will our children who farm in the future have to feed on that same land? As the number of people increases, pressure on the land intensifies. Will the land be able to handle the task? Will our children be able to meet the demand? It all depends on how well we take care of it now, while it's in our care—before we turn it over to the next generation of caretakers.

You know, God's not making any more land, and we cover up nearly three-quarters of a million acres each year in the United States with asphalt and concrete. That means we're going to have to try harder each year to take care of what's left. Most farmers take care of the land, but some aren't as careful. This is also true with other caretakers of the land, including our governments. Those who aren't careful with the land aren't necessarily bad folks—they often just don't think.

Earth Day: The Good and the Bad

I heard it again this evening on the six o'clock news, "It is now feared that the blasting may upset the ecology of the endangered Indiana bat." Well, the bats

As the number of people increases, pressure on the land intensifies. Will the land be able to handle the task? It all depends on how well we take care of it now, while it's in our care—before we turn it over to the next generation of caretakers. Summer grass, cured and preserved in these two round bales, will feed cattle during the winter while the farmer's pasture is dormant.

will probably be upset all right, but their ecology won't. "Ecology" is probably one of the most misused and misunderstood terms in today's language. It's easy to understand why. The news media, which sometimes portrays itself as on the cutting edge of correct grammar and enunciation, is riddled with incorrect applications of the word. The word "ecology" can be broken down into "eco," (the earth) and "ology" (the study of). So ecology means "study of the earth." In purest definition, ecology means the study of plants and animals, and their relation to each other and their environment.

Experts in the field of ecology have likewise been slandered—or at least misrepresented. For example, "ecologists today made another unsuccessful attempt to stop Project A." An ecologist is one who studies ecology, nothing more. An ecologist may be concerned with Project A, but the ecologist is not usually the one waving the flags, carrying the banners, or threatening lawsuits. An ecologist is one who *studies* the environment. An environmentalist is one who is concerned about the environment. This person may be slightly concerned, moderately concerned, or extremely concerned. The environmentalist may or may not understand much about the field of ecology. Often, an environmentalist has only a peripheral understanding, knowing just enough to become excited and reactive.

I heard a fellow down at the feed store the other day talking about "them environmentalists." It caused me to pause and think. What is an environmentalist—a person so neatly pigeon-holed as a radical, educated, but ignorant liberal, whose flag-waving threats of doom and destruction have halted, if not stopped progress, on all fronts?

Are you an environmentalist? Am I? Before you answer, picture in your mind two people you know who might make the following statements.

Person number one:

"The earth is on a course of destruction. The air will soon not be fit to breathe nor the water to drink. The greenhouse effect will end life as we know it. Channelization, pavement, and shopping centers are irreversible. Bottomland hardwoods and wetlands will soon be gone forever. Humanity's greed and ecological ignorance will spell its doom."

Person number two:

"I'm sick and tired of hearing this doomsday talk by these knee-jerk liberals who call themselves educated. I'm old enough to be their father and times are better now than they've ever been. The only reason they can march and rant and rave about the roof falling in is because they have a full belly and nothing else to do. I can still breathe, and the water I drink is still clean. I remember when times were hard, and I don't want to go back. No sir, things are great and getting better."

Obviously, these two people have extreme points of view. But (brace yourself), I believe they both can be considered environmentalists! *Funk and Wagnalls' Dictionary* defines "environment" as the "external circumstances, conditions, and things that affect the existence and development of an individual, organism, or group." And an "environmentalist" as "one who advocates preservation of the environment." Now, between the extreme points of view of the two people above, there is a whole spectrum of viewpoints. And most folks are environmentalists whose ideas fall somewhere between those two extremes. Most folks are confused about how they feel, because they hear so much conflicting information.

But the fact is, everyone wants clean air to breathe, clean water to drink, and wholesome food. And though they may not think about it much, talk about it much, or rant and rave about it much, everyone wants our children to have the same.

Nearly thirty years ago, very few people had even heard the word "ecology." For example, I received a B.S. degree in agriculture at a major university without ever hearing or reading the word—much less knowing what it meant. It wasn't until I attended graduate school that I first became aware of the enlightening and intriguing field of ecology. The public's first massive exposure to the word "ecology" came on "Earth Day," April 22, 1970, during a massive national educational campaign to make the general public aware of environmental problems in this country. Schools held classes and civic organizations had programs. Television and radio brought these concerns into the homes of millions of Americans. I'm sure the organizers of Earth Day had no idea the commotion that would follow, how long it would last, and how many changes it would cause.

I remember well the pandemonium that resulted in the weeks, months, and years that followed Earth Day 1970. As I look back on it now, I have to chuckle a little. It reminds me of hitting a stubborn mule in the head with a two-by-four to get his attention. Hundreds of causes sprang up, sit-ins and demonstrations were staged, and hasty laws were passed. Well-meaning but poorly informed citizens tried to correct complex problems overnight—ones that had evolved over decades of industrial and technological revolution. This resulted in creating polarized factions—the "environmentalists" and the "realists." Both had valid points of view, but they spent more time fighting each other than correcting the real problems of the day. The sad thing is, I believe that, deep down, they both wanted the same thing—a wholesome life for themselves and their children!

There is no doubt that concern for the environment has had a tremendous impact on our society. We needed to become aware. We had some real problems with our water, our air, and our soil. We had become accustomed to dumping our wastes into nature's systems with reckless abandon and without the thought that we would have to deal with them later. As an uninformed and unaware society, we were creating an environment unsafe and unpleasant to live in. Earth Day set this country on the road to cleaning up its mess. New laws, new policies, and a new understanding were being born.

The pendulum was swinging the other way, and it was good. But pendulums don't stop in the middle. They keep going beyond the reasonable to the other extreme. A little knowledge often tends to make people react before they learn the whole story. And when those concerned with our environment screamed too loud, too often, about issues of too little significance, the issues of major significance began to be ignored—the "cry wolf" syndrome. And the pendulum began to swing back the other way.

Life is full of compromises. There will always be disagreements, and a progressive society must learn to accommodate these disagreements. There are some things that are given—no question about it. First, there are certain events that will always occur under a given set of conditions. They have always happened and will continue to happen; we can depend on it. These are ecological principles. Second given: we must eat to live. And we must have clothes and shelter to protect us from the elements. If the masses in this world are to survive, we must use, to a certain degree, intensive agriculture and industry to feed them, clothe them, and provide their shelter. A perfect balance of nature will be hard to maintain under these conditions. This is not to say that we shouldn't work toward a balance, but we must understand that a pure balance cannot exist if the masses are to survive. Therefore, the reasonable sector of our society—those trained in ecological principles, and those who know how to feed, clothe and shelter the masses—must come together to help create a system that will do the job. But we must always keep a cautious eye on safeguarding the environment upon which we all depend.

As we approach the thirtieth anniversary of Earth Day, it's time to reflect. Most of the schoolchildren who sat in those classes in 1970 are now in their late thirties and early forties. The "environmentalists" and the "realists," though still polarized, are beginning to understand each other a little better, to work together a little more. And though there are still notable exceptions, newer environmental laws are beginning to make a little more sense. There seems to be more thought from both sides put into them before they're passed. I can't help but wonder about Earth Day 2010. I'd like to believe we'll all be working together even more—but then, I'm an optimist by nature.

Confusion of Conservation Terms Slows Progress

"Life is so simple, yet so complex." While at first glance that phrase seems contradictory, it truly reflects the range of human understanding. To a baby, life is simple—it's made up of food, warmth, comfort, light, and dark. To a molecular ecologist, each new discovery adds another layer of mystery to a world so complex it staggers the imagination. Some of us choose to look at the big picture, to sift through the volumes of detail to sort out simple concepts. Others spend a lifetime trying to unravel the minute details surrounding the life of one microscopic organism.

Yes, it depends how closely you look at it. As mentioned earlier, the term "ecology" can be defined as the study of the earth. The subject can be thoroughly covered in a fifteen-page 4-H pamphlet written on a sixth-grade level. Or it can occupy ten shelves of books in the library, most written at a level scientists need a bottle of aspirins to grasp.

Several years ago, I carried a vanload of students to a professional wildlife meeting in West Virginia. The opening session was a discussion of "biodiversity" by a panel of five national wildlife experts. Biodiversity in the last few years has been a popular buzzword in Washington. National symposia devoted to the topic are commonplace, and grant money on the subject abounds. The students all had a good grasp of the concept before they heard the panelists, but left the meeting totally confused. The reason? Because the panelists couldn't agree on what biodiversity means. In fact, more than one commented that before biodiversity can be seriously addressed, there would have to be agreement on a definition of the term. And they didn't visualize that happening for some time.

To me the concept is simple, but you have to understand—I think that way. Here's my 4-H definition. Biodiversity means "several plant and animal species living together." Here's my professional definition. Biodiversity means "a range in the number of species on a unit of land, between two and the maximum number that unit of land can support." In other words, a unit of land is biodiverse if it has at least two species. The *degree* of biodiversity is another matter. It depends on how many species are present compared to the maximum.

Another Washington buzzword is "sustainable agriculture." Seems simple enough to me: "food and fiber produced in ways that conserve natural resources." Old agricultural systems often resulted in soil erosion and poor water quality. Sustainable agriculture seems like a good idea, but we can't agree on the degree of natural resource loss or impairment we're willing to tolerate. Some have misconstrued the term to mean "low-input agriculture." In other words, little or no pesticides, inorganic fertilizer, or soil tillage. While these may contribute to sustainable agriculture, they don't mean the same thing. Since low-input agriculture techniques are controversial in some circles, this misconcept has slowed the acceptance of sustainable agriculture. I once attended a heated discussion of sustainable agriculture in a meeting of college agricultural deans. There's little wonder why the general public is confused, if professionals can't agree that producing food and fiber in ways that conserve natural resources is a good thing to do!

And then there's the term "wetlands." If you want to create a controversy, just mention the term in a meeting of land managers. We all know that wetlands conserve soil moisture, filter out environmental contaminants, and provide rich wildlife habitat, all noble endeavors. But natural resource professionals have carried wetlands conservation too far. Why? It goes back again to definition. My definition of wetlands is "an ecosystem comprising permanently saturated soils with associated plant and animal communities." In their haste to preserve this precious rapidly declining resource, agencies have defined wetlands in a multitude of ways. One extreme includes a bottomland forest that is sometimes (but seldom) covered with water. Another includes a field flooded by unnatural causes, such as a clogged culvert. Car-

Wetland—an ecosystem comprising permanently saturated soils with associated plant and animal communities. A thriving wetland, complete with beaver lodge, growing trees, and aquatic plants.

ried to this extreme, current wetlands conservation laws prevent land managers from managing land to its best use.

Common sense has taken the back seat to legal entanglement when it comes to land management. Our land is being managed in many cases by lawyers and judges, whose only land experience comes from laws passed by well-meaning but often misinformed legislators.

Yes, life is simple, but if we try hard enough and study it long enough, we can make it complex.

Renewable Natural Resources: What Does It Mean?

Speaking of terms, there's a lot of confusion about another important term—"renewable natural resource." Natural means *from nature*, and resource means *something useful*. The term "renewable" means being able to *renew itself*. So, if you put the three words together, "renewable natural resource" means something useful from nature that renews itself. It sounds simple only because it is. Some natural resources are not renewable, such as diamonds, petroleum, coal, etc. The renewable natural resources include things such as forests, wildlife, air, water, and fish. It's nice to think that we will never run out of these resources, but there's a catch! To be truly renewable, a natural resource must be managed. It must receive *a degree of* protection, even though it doesn't have to be totally protected and never used. In fact, the more a resource is used (if wisely), the better—at least for most renewable natural resources. Two more terms here: "Conservation" means *wise use*; preservation means *no use*. If we totally protect a deer herd, it would overpopulate, eat up its food supply, and large numbers of deer would die from disease, starvation, or harsh weather. If we didn't harvest wood products from the forest, trees would get old and decadent and hundreds of what otherwise would have been very usable trees would die and fall to the ground. Some say this is good, because we need to replenish the organic matter in the forest floor. We do, but we don't need that much! Natural pruning of limbs and shedding of leaves each year gives us enough organic matter, particularly when we add feces and decaying bodies of wild animals and plants.

We haven't always known how to manage and just how much protection is needed for these renewable natural resources. In fact, wildlife management didn't come into being until the early 1930s. One management tool we use today is regulating the harvest of game, so we harvest each year just what nature produces. Several game species almost bit the dust before we learned how to regulate hunting, to manipulate habitat, and to use other wildlife practices common today. Wildlife management has brought deer, turkey, elk, antelope, and many other species from near the brink of extinction to flourishing populations over much of the country. One species that didn't make it was the passenger pigeon. In the late 1800s, the passenger pigeon was one of the most abundant game species in the country. The U.S. Department of Interior estimated there were nine million passenger pigeons in the United States in 1850. It was not uncommon to see them in flocks as large as today's blackbird flocks. The difference between passenger pigeons and blackbirds is that the passenger pigeon was considered an excellent food source. As there were no hunting regulations, they were commonly killed by the thousands. Market hunters went into the roosting areas at night, slaying the birds and hauling them away by wagonloads to St. Louis, New Orleans, and other cities to be served in restaurants and hotels. They were also sold as food at local markets. These market hunters were not doing anything illegal; this was a commonly accepted practice back in those days. In order to save shotgun shells, they would pick a dense group and try to get several with one blast, and in the process they would leave several cripples, which were quickly consumed by house cats and other predators. The last passenger pigeon died, according to some sources, around 1914. Some people have blamed the demise of the passenger pigeon on habitat destruction. Even though that's the primary cause of wildlife decline today, the loss of the passenger pigeon was probably due more to overhunting than to any other factor. With today's game laws regulating how many, when, and how to harvest game species, we don't have to worry about hunting being responsible for wildlife extinction in this country—ever again.

Wetlands and Sick Rivers

Throughout the eastern United States, many river systems are sick. Years of abuse, trial and error at management, and court entanglement have left them in an awful mess—some are essentially nothing more than stagnant, unproductive, stopped-up sewers. I think we've arrived at a crossroads—a place in time to back off, look at what's happened, and set about to correct the problem. It's not that we haven't done anything at all. But until now our efforts have been short term, ill conceived, and artificial. I believe we have the know-how to work with nature to solve the problem. Let's take a look at two river systems in my home state which, I think, typify other systems throughout the eastern part of our country.

This article is not meant to be technical, but some explanation of process is important to make my point. I'll leave statistics to others—and deal more with concepts.

A lot of time, money, and energy have been devoted to legal definitions. The following definitions are mine, and I give them here to clarify my concepts. What is a wetland?—it's an ecosystem comprising permanently saturated soils with associated plant and animal communities. What is flooding?—it's a temporary covering of water after heavy rainfall. What is swamping out?—it's a prolonged flooding; standing water for long periods, killing trees and other plant life. Wetlands are alive and productive; swamped-out areas have little life and are unproductive.

What causes flooding?—it's when a drainage system is inadequate to absorb or carry off excessive rainfall, either by too little absorption in the watershed, or because of clogged waterways. Before agriculture, transportation, and urban development, we had no problem with flooding and swamping. We had absorptive forestland, and nothing to clog meandering waterways. Temporary floods were confined to the floodplain, and they receded quickly. Beavers lived here in harmony with the land; there was no excessive flooding nor swamping; we had live, thriving wetlands.

What happened? Clearing land for farming didn't cause excessive problems for over one hundred years. The farming methods were not so obtrusive and the system was forgiving. There were small fields and vegetative buffer strips to hold the soil. The industrial revolution began to take hold and more and more people left the farm, leaving fewer farmers to grow the nation's food. The remaining farmers compensated by clearing larger fields. A lack of education about how and why to prevent soil erosion resulted in removal of the absorptive forest cover, and siltation clogged waterways. Around World War II, when mule farming shifted to tractor farming, our methods became even more obtrusive. Meanwhile, more people were leaving the farm.

Recognizing the problems with soil erosion, the Soil Conservation Service (SCS) (now the National Resource Conservation Service [NRCS]) and the Agricultural Extension Service began working to educate farmers and help them reduce soil erosion. Contour farming, cover crops, strip cropping, and especially terracing were effective in turning the erosion problem around. A great deal of highly erodible land was taken out of row crops and reforested. In addition, approximately one million acres of land was terraced.

Beginning in the 1960s, though, much of the earlier soil-conservation work was neglected. Spiraling costs and government policy put added pressure on farmers to produce more to "feed the world." Larger machinery (some capable of planting twelve rows at a pass) became common. Terraces were plowed down for the convenience of the large equipment. Fences were torn down to make fields larger, and contour farming was abandoned. Meanwhile, fewer and fewer farmers were feeding more and more people. To complicate matters, tenant farmers with short-term leases tended to ignore conservation practices, because they cost money and had no short-term economic benefit. On these lands, no one was assuming stewardship. Soil erosion once more became a serious problem for West Tennessee. As the sixties turned into the seventies, the industrial world discovered new uses for soybeans, and prices shot upward. Now that fewer farmers were farming and larger, more efficient equipment was available, row-crop farming boomed. This prompted clearing more bottomland forest and converting erodible pasture and forest land to cropland. Erosion rates soared.

As the meandering waterway system clogged with silt, local drainage districts, as early as 1912, began to channelize the streams. In 1948 Congress authorized the West Tennessee Tributaries Project—a project to channelize the Obion and Forked Deer Rivers. In 1972 the Obion-Forked Deer River Basin Authority was created by the Tennessee General Assembly to clean out existing channels and build silt-retention lakes in the watershed.

Because of public concern over the channelization work, it never was completed. The first lawsuit was filed April 23, 1970. It took three years, but eventually channelization came to a halt. The legal battles intensified for over twenty-five years, resulting in on-again, off-again work. Meanwhile, as the years passed by, soil erosion accelerated, and the problem worsened. In recent years, no-till crop production techniques, Conservation Reserve Program (CRP) provisions of the 1985 Farm Act, and numerous watershed lakes have tremendously reduced the erosion rate. The farm economy slump in the early eighties also resulted in less erosion. Now soil erosion is more under control, but our drainage problem is getting worse every year. Why? *Because we couldn't agree* on how to correct the problem created years ago!

Channelization doesn't seem to be the answer. Conservationists suspected that for a long time. Finally, a report in 1982 by the U.S. Geological Survey confirmed it. Long, meandering natural waterways were designed by the good Lord to carry water off slowly. Straight, deep channelized ditches were designed by humans to carry it off fast. Time has shown that nature rejects this idea. As the early channels were dug, they worked at first—for a little while. Just long enough to dry out the floodplain—bottomland and low-lying areas—to a point of false security. As economic incentives increased, farmers cleared bottomland forest to capture some of the newly dried-out land for more crops. People began to expand housing out into the low-lying, formerly swamped-out areas.

But it didn't last long. Young trees of rapidly growing species had taken root on the spoil banks left after digging the straight ditches. As the channels carried water off faster, the current rapidly eroded the banks, undercutting tree roots and causing the trees to topple into the channels. Some washed downstream and lodged against others still held in place by a few roots, causing (over time) massive log jams. Before long these obstructions began to slow the water enough to cause silt and sand to settle out. It didn't take long for the channelized ditches to fill up with silt, sand, and fallen trees.

One handy place for these debris jams to occur was at bridges, where pilings blocked the downstream progress of the uprooted trees. These jams slowed the water in the center of the ditches and forced even faster flow around the edges, where it began to undermine the bridge abutments. In recent years well-traveled highway bridges have collapsed, and others have been classified as dangerous.

As the channels filled with silt and trees, the water began to spread farther and farther across the land and stay longer and longer after each rain. Channel levees actually kept floodwaters from receding. In time, fertile hardwood bottoms and cropland became permanently swamped out. Trees which could live quite well while flooded in the winter dormant season when most of the rainfall occurs, now died from being flooded during the growing season, too. They had already been stressed by silt and sand deposition.

Meanwhile, beavers, which had not been present in several decades, began to make a comeback. In the early sixties a beaver was a novelty in West Tennessee. By the mid-seventies they were common. Why? Not because they were restocked, but because habitat conditions were perfect—there was plenty of water, along with young, fast-growing trees associated with the channel spoil banks. Beavers prefer the bark of fast-growing species. With sometimes large but often small check dams in strategic places, the beavers could hold water on the swamped-out areas even longer, thus further complicating the problem.

As the legal battles raged on, the situation worsened. Water crept farther and farther from the channels, higher and higher into surrounding areas. Land, once never flooded, became temporary floodplains, then permanent floodplains—then became permanently swamped out. Roads, airports, homes, and businesses, even those not built in the floodplains—some were over forty years old and had never been flooded—were now being flooded regularly.

I grew up near Trenton, in the Forked Deer basin. In the forties and fifties we farmed in the Forked Deer riverbottom, not right up to the river, but just out of the annual floodplain. The land belonged to Mr. Lige Parker, and we were sharecroppers. In the late fifties, the land we farmed began to flood, infrequently at first, then more frequently. After a while, it permanently swamped out, and for many years was just ponded water, devoid of life for all practical purposes. Today, it is still swamped out, and the water keeps creeping up onto the surrounding land. Mr. Parker's grandson pays taxes on all the land, but has less and less to farm each year. The Trenton livestock sale barn, where I always took my hogs, began to flood on a regular basis, as did the airport which I watched being built in the early sixties. Other natives of the West Tennessee area—those who know and love the land—can relate many similar experiences.

The values of wetlands are well documented. They reduce flood damage, recharge groundwater, filter sediment, abate pollution, and provide wildlife habitat, among other things. Ecologists have understood wetlands and the value they hold for a long time. They sounded the alarm for years that our nation's wetlands were being wiped out at an alarming rate. Fifty-six percent of the original wetland acreage has been lost. But no one would listen. Most (92 percent) of the remaining wetlands are in private ownership. The importance of the agricultural industry to this country and the vital role of America in feeding the world insulated American farmers from the concern of ecologists. However, as the nation's public became better educated, especially through television, it finally heard the urgent pleas ecologists had been making for years. Suddenly, wetlands were no longer wastelands, but areas of vital national interest, more important in some respects than oil.

As the nation became more and more concerned with increased water pollution and the loss of wetlands, a rash of laws were enacted to protect the nation's remaining wetlands. These laws in recent years have been enforced to limit activities of those whose job it is to bring the West Tennessee drainage problem under control. Not only was wetland destruction halted, but so was drainage of other lands covered with water—any water—all water. So we've gone from one extreme to another—from total drainage of all water-covered land, including valuable wetlands, to no drainage of any land covered with water, including swamped-out land once productive as cropland and bottomland forests.

Soon the battle lines were drawn. Proponents of both sides carried the banners and made the headlines. As the years passed, the positions of both parties hardened. In this modern day of educational enlightenment and communications, instead of coming together in arbitration, the two groups further polarized. Trust no longer prevailed, if it ever did. Instead of arbitration, the legal battle intensified in the state legislature.

Meanwhile, the rest of us either watched or joined sides. Any statement of concern about wetlands brought the risk of being pigeonholed as "environmentalist" or "duck hunter." Any statement of concern about the rights of landowners brought the label "farmer" or "anti-conservationist." Both parties blamed someone else—usually each other—but scapegoats such as hunters and beavers were blamed as well. Beavers certainly don't help the problem, but they are simply a byproduct of our poor management and legal entanglement. Any attempt at mediation brought a squint of the eye and the question—asked or unasked—whose side are you on?

The sad part was that both parties meant well and wanted to do the right thing. The sad part was that every single person involved loved the land. The sad part was that we have the technology to solve the problem. The sad part was that we are all intelligent, civilized people, and everyone was losing this war—landowners *and* the general public.

Common sense would dictate that wise stewardship of any river system should include a floodplain whose integrity is enforced. Floodplain of the Forked Deer River in West Tennessee.

The root of the problem is soil erosion. Though not completely under control, it's not nearly the problem it was. No-till agriculture, CRP provisions of the Farm Act, and watershed lakes already built by the Obion–Forked Deer River Basin Authority (now the West Tennessee River Basin Authority) have severely curtailed the amount of sediment washing into the system. Our principal task is to unravel the problems created by yesterday's poor management. Once we correct that, we should have the system under control.

The biggest challenge in solving the problem was a policy issue. And that was the question of what the end result should be. Which land should be preserved as wetlands and which should be restored to productive status as cropland or bottomland forest? Which land should be restored and protected as floodplain? Common sense would dictate that wise stewardship of any river system should include a floodplain whose integrity is enforced. And, finally, how do we compensate landowners for any losses they incur when their land is needed for public benefit? Several programs already exist for providing compensation, such as the U.S. Department of Interior's Small Wetlands Acquisition Program, the USDA's Water Bank, and the wetland acquisition program of the Tennessee Wildlife Resources Agency (TWRA). The concept of a Permanent Wetland Reserve was discussed in a USDA report released in August 1990.

Once we agreed on these policy issues, the next step was to agree on the technology to get the job done. Restoring the old meandering river system, snagging and clearing, building long low bridges across wide bottoms instead of long road dams that block the flow, and beaver control are just a few of the technologies that would begin to restore the integrity of our basin. In short, the plan was to remove from the floodplain all levees, dams, or other devices that impede water flow. The task—by working with, instead of against nature—was to restore the river system to a manageable condition. We've tried to conquer the natural world and failed. Nature will provide for us and even allow us to manage her to provide our needs. But she will not be dominated.

Fortunately, after a year-long debate by a group representing all interests, a sensible plan was developed to restore the integrity of the river systems. At this writing, the project awaits federal funding for the U.S. Army Corps of Engineers to carry it out. Common sense prevailed—and we should hope that funding will soon be forthcoming. Meanwhile, the water problem is getting worse every year. The water keeps rising and the bridges keep falling.

On Ethics

I always look forward to my daily run. Obviously, it's good to get the heart pumping again and to dissipate lactic acid from inactive muscles. But it's also an opportunity to clear the cobwebs out of my head after a tough day in the office—to get things back into perspective.

One day at the office, on two or three occasions, I was asked to mediate in questions of ethics. My run that afternoon helped me sort them out. I don't know which was racing faster—my heart, my legs, or my mind. Come to think of it, it must've been my heart or my mind. My legs went about normal pace, but one thing's for sure: the run was over before I knew it. And if I could have written this while running, my pen couldn't have kept up with my mind.

These days we often hear the term ethics used in association with natural resources. Hunting ethics, land ethics, outdoor recreation ethics, etc.—all roll off the end of our tongues. But ethics (or the lack of it) is found in all human endeavors. I have to chuckle as I'm reminded of what a friend asked me several years ago, when he'd heard I'd been offered an administrative job. "Jim," he said, "how're you going to handle the politics? You know that administrators have to deal in politics all the time, and you don't seem to be the type." "Well," I told him, "I don't see anything wrong with politics. In fact, it's a very credible field—you can even get a college degree in the study of it—political science. What's wrong with that?" I had him going and I knew it. He was flustered. "You know what I mean, Jim—the kind of politics where you rub my back and I'll rub yours, whether it's right or not."

Fact is, Ron had fallen into the age-old trap of pigeon-holing. The same thing most of us do every day. We constantly see in the news media the worst side of politicians in elected public office. And, politicians practice politics—so politics must be bad. First of all, the media practically never show us the *good side* of politicians. But I'm convinced the good *far outweighs* the bad. The good *does not make* news though. *Funk and Wagnall's Dictionary* is even confused about politics. In part of the definition, such glowing adjectives as "skillful, ingenious, wise and prudent" are used. Further on, politics is described as "The acts or practices of those who seek any position of power or advantage." Actually, I define politics in one word: "networking." And networking is the ability to make friends among people in many walks of life and effectively working with them to get things done.

But the fact is, it all comes down to ethics. We have ethical politicians, unethical politicians, and a whole range in between. Lawyers fit the same scenario. I've heard enough lawyer jokes in the last few years to fill a book. But the practice of law is a needed profession. It helps maintain order in a very complex society. If you want to see the effect of living with little law and lawyers, go to some Third World countries. It can be chaotic! At least compared to the United States. Perhaps our country didn't need lawyers as badly in colonial days, but believe me we need them now. Don't get me wrong. I get just as aggravated as you do when I see unethical lawyers, and folks trying to take advantage of the legal system or of the uneducated. Million-dollar back settlements and "pain and suffering" suits are often hard for me to rationalize. But let's not pigeon-hole all politicians and all lawyers. As long as these two careers are practiced ethically, they are legitimate—and necessary.

Now, let's look at the term "ethics." In keeping with my philosophy of simple definitions, ethics means "responsibility to do what's right." There are moral ethics, business ethics, personal ethics, conservation ethics, and so on. The problem is that not everybody agrees about what's right. Such is the root of many of our problems. What's right usually comes down to what's fair, and opinion about what's fair varies, depending on your background. There's one thing for sure. You can't have a credible opinion about what's right until you've heard both sides. And before you can hear both sides, you *have to listen!* Sound elementary? It is. But so often, a common reason settlements can't be reached is that the two parties won't listen to each other. A good politician is one who listens to both sides before acting—and then acts for the *right reason:* what's right, instead of what will get him or her reelected, or what will get him or her the most money or advantage.

I believe it was Davy Crockett who said, "Be sure you're right—then go ahead." Good advice. And don't worry about who else thinks it's right. What *you* think—that's what's most important. Even so, a wise person will listen to the opinion of others.

What motivates people to act ethically? Unfortunately, for some it takes laws and enforcement—punishment, in other words. Others are motivated by a clear conscience. Some are motivated by approval of their peers or a pat on the back from someone they respect. Others are motivated by peace of mind. As a general rule, though, the older a person is, the harder it is to motivate him or her. So we have to reach the kids. Kids are motivated by simple ideals. What's right is right. That's all there is to it! You take care of the land because it's the right thing to do—for yourself *and* for future generations. You know, we could learn a lot from our kids. . . .

Agriculture and the Environment: Progress Is Being Made

We're blessed to live in a part of the world where the air is still relatively safe to breathe and the water safe to drink. This isn't true in all parts of the world. My trips to other countries have heightened my awareness about how precious these commodities are to us—and how fortunate we are in the United States to be able to walk up to a public water fountain without worry.

Often we feel we must have some things we *really can* do without—cars, TV, and our favorite music. These are nice, but when you really get down to it, in addition to clean air and water, we must have food, clothing, and shelter. That's it. And all of these are products of agriculture.

Agriculture, as we all know, has accomplished the modern miracle. In the face of a mushrooming world population (it's doubled in my lifetime—and I don't consider myself an old man!), a shrinking land base to build roads and housing, and fewer and fewer farmers (only 2 percent of us in the United States farm now), we have more food, clothing, and shelter than ever before. Now that's a miracle by anybody's measure!

How can we do it? Because of modern technology through research and education—and because nearly 20 percent of the workforce supports our precious few farmers. How long can this miracle last—how far can we go? Nobody knows, but we do know that U.S. agriculture, which leads the pack throughout the world, must continue to produce bright young scientists to develop this technology. We need to develop technology that will not only keep our declining land resource productive, but preserve environmental integrity at the same time. Declining enrollments in agriculture programs throughout U.S. colleges and universities are disturbing. We are gradually

Agriculture has created the modern miracle. In the face of a mushrooming world population, fewer farmers, and a shrinking land base, we have more food, clothing, and shelter than ever before. Holstein cattle on a Tennessee dairy farm, next to a subdivision.

losing our brain trust in the nation's most vital industry. But that's another story for another day.

As the population grows and people crowd closer together, we must be more and more careful about environmental degradation. Our increased agricultural production by fewer farmers on less land to feed more people has caused us to need larger equipment, more pesticides, and more fertilizer—in short, our practices have placed more pressure on our land and water, and more tendency for pollution. While the U.S. public is becoming more vigilant about environmental pollution (in 1990, we spent $115 billion for pollution control, four times what we spent in 1972), American agriculture has become more vigilant, too. Let's look at some of the things U.S. agriculture is doing to clean its stables.

Pesticides. Over the last several years, research has developed alternative, target-specific pesticides with shorter life—ones that hit the pest quickly and break down in a few days. We continue to develop biological agents to control pests—such as viruses, bacteria, fungi, and predatory insects. We are learning how to manipulate the habitat to encourage natural pest pathogens. Through integrated pest management (IPM), we are combining pest-control tools, monitoring pest populations, and spraying pesticides only when we must to keep pest populations at levels below economic thresholds. This saves money and protects the environment, too. Through biotechnology, we are combining genetic material of plants and animals to control pests. For example, if a bacterium kills a bug that eats tomatoes, we can transplant genetic material from the bacterium to the tomato plant, so the tomato can protect itself.

Soil Erosion. Conservation tillage has reduced soil erosion, while maintaining soil moisture and organic matter. Terraces, sod waterways, and soil-retention dams have been saving soil, improving water quality and saving farmers money for some time. Since the Conservation Reserve Program (CRP) began in 1985, the average soil loss per acre on these lands has been reduced from 21 tons per acre to 1.6 tons per acre.

Production and Processing Wastes. We have been using the anaerobic bacterial action of lagoons for years to keep animal production wastes out of our streams. Solids from the lagoons are used as mulch, and liquids are used as fertilizer for the land. We are recycling some of these liquids through catfish production units. We are beginning to see water hyacinths used in lagoons to take up excess nutrients.

We are studying ways to recycle food-processing wastes back through livestock as feed. We are also using manure and other organic biomass to generate heat.

Water Quality. By keeping soil and wastes out of our streams, we are not only improving water quality, but also saving money for farmers as well. In recent years we've discovered a problem with excess nitrates in ground water—a result of nitrogen fertilizer. Through biotechnology, we are finding ways to grow crops with less nitrogen fertilizer. For example, we're trying to combine genetic material of legumes (such as soybeans) with that of nonlegumes (such as corn) so we can develop nonlegumes that will capture their own nitrogen from the air.

Agricultural Research to Combat Non-Agricultural Pollution. Not only is agriculture cleaning up its own act, it's working on ways to clean up non-agricultural pollution. One exciting area is the study and development of soil microbes which tie up soil toxicants (heavy metals from human sewage sludge, for example) to keep them from being uptaken by plants which people and animals eat. Through genetic engineering, we are developing different strains of microbes to degrade different kinds of pollution, such as oil spills. We are also finding ways to increase soil microbe effectiveness, such as fertilizing them.

There are many sources of environmental pollution in our modern culture. And while there's no doubt that agriculture has caused its share, it's making progress to remedy the problem. In the process, it's still feeding and clothing the people of the world—pretty remarkable, I'd say!

Forests of the Future

What will our forests be like in the future? How much will we have? What will they look like? Once we know what we want, it's simple enough to make them that way through land management. Problem is, we can't agree on what we want. Different folks who use the forest need different things from it, all of which are legitimate, but not all are compatible. Here's some straight talk: it's hard for a forest to provide pulpwood and red-cockaded woodpecker habitat at the same time. Turkey hunting and ATVs don't go together so well either.

Of all the things our forests provide us, which are the most important? Good question. We could ask the same about our cars. Which is most important, the engine or the wheels? They both must be important, because the car won't function without either. Fact is, all parts of the forest are important, too, and all products and services it renders are valuable—whether or not we can easily hang a price tag on it. Folks who wave banners for hiking, aesthetics, peace, and solitude have a point. Folks who stubbornly contend that forests should provide wood are right too. Where else will it come from? And somewhere in between, the folks who want harvestable populations of game and, yes, even ATV trails—all have a legitimate vested interest.

But there are two important howevers here—*big* howevers. First, the more products and services we take out of the forest, the better job we must do to manage it, if we expect it to continue to be productive on a sustained basis. And the more different things we take out at the same time, the harder the forest is to manage. Second, there's no way we can all use a tract of forest at the same time—no way. If you've ever tried to turkey hunt during an ATV convention, you know what I mean.

So what's the answer? I think we can all have the nation's forests our way, but we can't have all the nation's forests our way. In other words, we have to manage our forestland to its highest and best use, as determined by the landowner. That primary use should dictate the management regime we use for that tract of land. There will always be many other secondary uses that will be more or less compatible. Whenever demand for a particular use becomes great enough, as determined by the market place, it will then become the primary use, and the management scenario will change.

Some folks will think I'm crazy for saying such a thing—that recreation will go down the drain. Not so. There are already a number of instances around the country where hunting fees are netting landowners much more than wood products. And when hiking, birdwatching, and solitude become important enough to us, we'll pay. This is already the case with a few forest areas of the northeastern United States—forests sprinkled amidst dense human populations. Public lands set aside for recreation buffer the cold hard cash reality, too.

There's an important catch to my philosophy. The forest can provide all these things for all these folks, but so far all we've mentioned are luxuries. Now let's talk survival. The forest provides a few things we must have, such as oxygen and clean water—water clean enough to drink. Clean enough because it was detained long enough to filter through the forest canopy, down through the porous forest soil into underground aquifers. So, no matter what the use, no matter what management tool we employ, we have an obligation to ourselves, to one another, and to the Lord who owns it but put us in charge, to use the forest wisely—and with respect. For example, Tennessee has developed a set of Best Management Practices the state recommends for logging and other forestry operations. We should develop a similar set of recommended practices for each forest use and support a vigorous education program to implement them. And as much as I hate regulation, if it's needed to protect the land, so be it. Our society is too complex, and we are all too dependent on the land to allow any individual to abuse it. We don't live in the pioneer days anymore.

OK, you say, even if we assume this philosophy for private lands, what about public land? I believe the same principle should apply—the landowner should determine the highest and best use, and all other uses should be secondary. Problem is, we're all owners of our public land, and we all not only want a piece of the cake—we all want the center piece with the cherry on top. Fortunately, we taxpayers own many kinds of public land. Some are set aside primarily for recreation, some for wildlife, and some for timber. Some is owned by all U.S. citizens, some by state citizens, and some by local citizens. We taxpayers bought the land, decided what its primary uses would be, and hired competent natural resource professionals to manage it for us. We own enough cakes that if we as individuals can't get the piece with the cherry from one cake, we can get it from another.

While we're fighting over our own special piece of the cake, we each try to get our natural resource professionals to take our side. We try to get them to cut our piece to fit our own selfish interest. But, in some ways, as citizens we're much like a board of directors of a company. We decide as a group what's best for the company—and this will in turn help all of us, not any particular member who may have a selfish interest. Collectively, we're the boss, and we should be—we own the company. But any good board is going to let the employees, who collectively know most about the company, make the daily decisions. The board should always have ultimate veto and approval authority. But as long as the company is turning out the right kind of widgets, it's best to let the employees do the jobs they know best. We the public have already—based on demand—decided what the primary uses of each of our public lands will be. We should continue to monitor the natural resource professionals. But let's not try to micromanage them, because they know their jobs best.

OK, I'll admit that in the past, some of our natural resource professionals were narrowly trained. They knew how to manage one resource well, but didn't know much about the others. But this is changing. Today's professional is coming out of college with a better understanding of the whole cake.

So what will our future forests look like? We can all speculate. I don't know what they'll be like, but I'll tell you what I hope they'll be like. I hope they'll be a mosaic of different aged forests, which will provide us with a multitude of products and services. I hope they're managed well by competent professionals. I hope we the public keep every square inch we have, and even buy more. And I hope the private forests are profitable, because if they're not, someday they won't be forests.

Final Thoughts

The Vision

Last night, I had a dream—a vision, actually, of a system within a system. The smaller system was living off the other—taking from it but not putting back. Most units of the smaller system didn't understand the larger system at all. All units drew regularly from the larger system, but too few put too little back. In the beginning, the small system was simple and natural, but as it grew it became more artificial and complex. The units eventually lost touch with the larger natural mother system. The artificial system grew and grew, drawing more and more resources from the mother—gradually consuming her from inside out.

As the passageway between the two systems became smaller, more and more resources had to pass through it. The units became more dependent on the growing artificial system, because they knew less and less about the larger. But ironically all the resources needed by the artificial system came through the narrow passageway.

Eventually, the mother system was totally consumed, and the shell crumbled away to ash, casting the now large artificial system out into a void to fend for itself—as if in birth. But unlike birth, it had no place to go except out into the universe. It no longer had a life-support system, and the universe was not kind and loving as the mother system had been. It quickly perished. Society is but a fetus in the womb of mother earth, and we are in mid-gestation.

The Reality

As I stated before, most people in the United States and in many other parts of the world are at least two generations removed from the land. Our agricultural system is so effective that less than 2 percent of our people farm. Many of the rest don't understand the land and its processes and aren't aware how dependent we are on it. As our society grows in complexity, it likewise grows in artificiality. Many of our children really think food comes from the store, and for those of us who know better, that awareness is dulled more each year. We're so well fed, clothed, and sheltered that our connection to the land is simply "out of sight, out of mind."

The more complex our society becomes and the faster our population increases, the more dependent on the land we become. It's ironic and sad that the more we become dependent on the land, the less we understand it. Even efforts to create awareness among our children have often resulted in a hands-on/preservation perspective, rather than a wise-use/conservation one. A growing number of people actually believe we shouldn't manage land resources—that we should leave them alone. After all, they seem to reason, we get our food, clothing, and shelter from the store. And because there's plenty now, surely that will continue.

If society is the fetus, our agricultural system is the umbilical cord. Through that living cord, we receive all the food, clothing, and shelter we need to live. For 99 percent of the time humans have existed, we all had a part in gathering our life needs. Then the cord was short, wide, and direct. But today that cord is long, convoluted, narrow, and shrinking every year. More of our precious few farmers are dropping out than are being replaced. Our U.S. land base to produce food and fiber is decreasing each year to make way for the growing infrastructure needed for our increasing society—roads, subdivisions, malls, and more. Through efforts by our land grant and state universities, improved agricultural efficiency has stayed ahead of demand, and that has given the appearance that we'll never run out of food and fiber. Resources are moving through the umbilical cord faster and more efficiently than ever, but that cord is shrinking, and the fetus it's feeding continues to grow.

This I Believe

There are many things I don't know, and many I never will. There are other things I suspect—some I may be able to verify before I die, and some I won't. But there are some things I firmly believe—with a confidence, with a conviction unwavering.

I believe there is a power greater than humans, who designed this miracle we call life, and the land which supports it. How can one witness the miracle of birth, see the likeness of the young to the parents, know that the genetic blueprint is only vaguely understood by humans, the highest life form on the planet, and not believe in a supreme power? How can one witness the spark of life, that elusive distinction between matter and living creatures, that flickers but survives through the greatest of odds, and know that although humans can recombine matter, they can't create the spark—and then not believe in a greater power? Surely doubters don't know and love the land.

I believe that no matter how much humans learn about life, the few miracles we unlock will only be a fraction of the many we never will. As a scientist and educator for most of my life, I have been inquisitive, and I have studied the inquiries of others. I continue to marvel that for every ecological truth we discover, we uncover a dozen new questions. The only thing that rivals our accumulation of knowledge is the realization of how ignorant we really are about the infinite number of things to know about the earth and how it works.

I believe that one of God's greatest gifts to us is not the land, but the stewardship of it, the right to use it—with love and respect. As perhaps the highest form of life, we humans have been given the thinking ability to harness natural systems to make great impact on our habitat. He has given us this brain tool, a powerful force that can cause mountains to be transformed and climates to modify. But this gift carries awesome responsibility, for should we use it unwisely, we will make the land unfit—not only for ourselves and our children, but for all the rest of His creations.

I believe that all parts of the land and all its creatures are equally important—that they deserve our care and respect—because they are all handicrafts of God and have a purpose, whether or not we understand it. How can we presume that we, only one species He has created, are more important than the several million others He has created? We have but one niche to fill in this earth machine. And though the steering wheel is an important part of the car, the carburetor air screw is important, too. The machine simply won't work right without all its parts.

I believe that humans cannot destroy the earth—we can only foul it, for ourselves, for other creatures, and for our children. Nothing humanity has ever conceived, or ever will conceive, can destroy the earth. In fact, the earth is close to indestructible. It has survived ice ages, re-arrangement of continents, shifting of seas, and comet collisions far more devastating than humans' puny nuclear arsenals. Nature continually heals our mistakes. The earth's marvelous system of biofilters cleanse our water and air, and we continually have to keep natural plant succession from reclaiming parking lots and buildings. Where we have relaxed our diligence, entire villages have reverted to forest.

I believe that the greatest hope of correcting our past environmental mistakes

Adults are hard to teach. Not so with children—they are inquisitive and eager to learn. An unidentified youngster ponders something of interest.

Final Thoughts

is to enlighten and encourage our children—before they learn instead our careless and wasteful ways. Once again, adults are hard to teach. Not so children—they are inquisitive and eager to learn, if the message is presented in an exciting way. They learn not only what we tell them, but even better when we show them. If we show them the wrong way, they learn that, too. The fact is, children grow up, and it doesn't take long. It takes a lot less effort to teach our children, and before you know it, they're the ones running things.

These things I believe, but finally this I know—that I'm thankful for my life, and for my relationship with the land. For I am a part of the living land, and it is a part of me. I have never been separated from the land, physically nor mentally, and I pray I never will.

Close to the Land was designed and typeset on a Macintosh computer system using PageMaker software. The text is set in Adobe Caslon, and the titles in Decoratura. This book was designed by Todd Duren, composed by Kimberly Scarbrough, and manufactured by Thomson-Shore, Inc. The recycled paper used in this book is designed for an effective life of at least three hundred years.